Sacred Rage

Sacred Rage

Love That Didn't Die with Them

BY
Damien W. D. Davis

FOREWORD BY
Sharon Okoh Davis

WIPF & STOCK · Eugene, Oregon

SACRED RAGE
Love That Didn't Die with Them

Wipf & Stock
An Imprint of Wipf and Stock Publishers
199 W. 8th Ave., Suite 3
Eugene, OR 97401

www.wipfandstock.com

PAPERBACK ISBN: 979-8-3852-5635-8
HARDCOVER ISBN: 979-8-3852-5636-5
EBOOK ISBN: 979-8-3852-5637-2

VERSION NUMBER 08/29/25

For Brooklyn "Boogie" Davis
You came into this world carrying my name,
my spirit, and my dreams.
You left this world carrying my heart.
You were—and still are—the joy that danced through our home,
the strength that rose even when your body was weak,
the laughter that lit up even the darkest days.
You taught me that fragile hands can still praise,
that broken hearts can still love,
and that even in suffering, there is beauty worth fighting for.
Every rainbow, every beam of sunlight,
every fierce moment of hope—
I see you.
You are not just a memory.
You are a promise:
that love outlives death,
that strength outshines sorrow,
and that joy is never truly lost.
This book is my offering to your memory,
my testimony to your light,
my vow that your name will echo across eternity.
Until we meet again, Boogie—
Daddy loves you forever.
You were the sparkle in glitter-covered crafts,
the giggle in bedtime stories,
the fierce hug after scraped knees.
I still hear your "I love you more" whispered in the silence.
You are not gone, Brooklyn.
You are the rhythm of my breath, the echo of every heartbeat.
This book is for you, Boogie.

Death is inevitable
Life is eternal
Love is free
Hatred costs
And everything is else subject to vanity

—*Rev. Dr. Damien W. D. Davis*

Contents

Foreword

"Blessed are those who mourn, for they will be comforted."

—MATTHEW 5:4 NIV

There are no words that can fully describe the heartbreak of losing a child. It is a grief so deep, so sacred, that it changes you forever. Since the passing of our daughter Brooklyn, my husband and I have walked a path marked by sorrow, love, confusion, faith, and sacred rage. Rage that rises not from hate, but from love that refuses to disappear in daily waves of grief. Rage rooted from the love that remains amidst the challenging reality of physical separation from our daughter.

When Damien shared with me that he was writing this book, I knew immediately it wasn't just a journal of thoughts—it was an offering.

> An offering to every grieving heart that has sat in silence, wondering how to continue leading life without their loved one.

> An offering to every grieving heart unsure if their pain was too loud, or too quiet, for the world to hear.

> An offering to every grieving heart that ever wondered if God had turned away in their suffering.

An offering to every grieving heart who has felt that they had to move on, as if the depth of their love had an expiration date.

This book, *Sacred Rage*, is a dependable companion for anyone navigating the unpredictable and often lonely road of grief. Through Scripture, reflection, and raw honesty, it reminds us that our emotions are not only valid but holy. It tells us that God does not require us to hide our pain or package it neatly. The peace of God is with us—in our tears, our questions, our silence, and even in our sacred rage.

> "Peace I leave with you; my peace I give you. I do not give to you as the world gives. Do not let your hearts be troubled and do not be afraid."
>
> —John 14:27 NIV

I believe this book is more than a resource—it's a lifeline. It gives people permission to feel what they feel, for as long as they need to. It gently pushes back on the idea that grief has a timeline or a proper appearance. *Sacred Rage* offers open-minded views that can escort the reader into a realm of sacred survival—surviving a life where each passing day feels further away from the memories you cherish of your loved one, leaving you stuck, wondering how to make it through the day and knowing that you cannot create new memories with them. The rage you experience to keep memories and love alive is shared in the pages of this book.

It acknowledges that love doesn't end, and neither should the memories or mentions of the ones we've lost.

Sacred Rage is a compassionate and faith-based resource, encouraging deep reflection on one's innermost emotions while offering the comfort and strength of God's word.

May *Sacred Rage* be a safe space for your soul. May it give voice to what your heart has been carrying in silence. And may it remind you, as it has reminded me, that there is beauty in remembrance, strength in vulnerability, and healing in honesty.

"I have told you these things, so that in me you may have peace. In this world you will have trouble. But take heart! I have overcome the world.""

—John 15:33 NIV

May God be with you and comfort you.

Sharon Okoh Davis

August 10, 2025

Preface

There are books that come from research and reflection—and then there are books that are written with a trembling hand and a shattered heart. This is the latter.

I did not set out to author a book on grief. I set out to survive it.

When our daughter Brooklyn passed, time stopped. The world tilted. The air grew heavier. And language—the tool I had relied on my entire life—failed me. What could I say that hadn't already been screamed in prayer or sobbed into the silence? What words could reach into that abyss and come back with something holy?

This book is my attempt to answer that question. It is part theology, part testimony. It is the intersection of sacred texts and sacred wounds, of lament and love, of faith that does not always look like praise. It is a witness to the coexistence of rage and reverence, doubt and devotion.

Grief, I have learned, is not a detour on the spiritual path—it is the path. Especially the kind of grief that comes when you lose a child. Especially when the world expects you to move on, to be strong, to make sense of the senseless. But sacred grief is not about resolution—it's about reverence. Sacred rage is not about blasphemy—it's about bearing witness to love that didn't die with them.

Brooklyn is not just the reason I drafted this book—she is written on every page. In every breathless pause, in every Scripture reread through tears, in every sentence where pain and praise share the same line. This is not a manual for fixing grief. It is a map of sacred ground.

I wrote it for the parent sitting in the back pew, too broken to sing. For the pastor who doesn't know what to say. For the friend who keeps showing up, even when it's awkward. For the faith leader who is trying to hold space for the unspeakable. And most of all, for those walking with empty arms and sacred memories—who need to know they are not alone.

You won't find answers in these pages. But you may find language. And that's where the work begins—not in conquering grief but in honoring it.

Brooklyn, this book is for you. It is my vow that your name will echo, that your light will burn, and that your love will never be silenced.

Some days I could only write a paragraph. Some days I couldn't write at all. But through tears, I kept returning to these pages—because her name deserved to be spoken, again and again. This book is not just my grief in ink; it is the rhythm of my breath and the cry of a father determined not to let silence bury love.

Acknowledgments

T his book was not written in isolation. It is the product of sacred conversations, sleepless nights, honest questions, and the courageous love that remains when all else has been taken.

To my daughter Brooklyn "Boogie" Davis—this is your echo on every page. Your absence is a wound, but your presence is eternal. You taught me how to listen with my soul and speak from the hollowed places of love.

To Sharon, my beloved wife—you have held my brokenness with grace, cradled my silence without demand, and stood beside me when grief tried to swallow us whole. You are the theology I live before I ever preach it.

To Josiah and Macy—your laughter is my resistance, your innocence is my reminder, and your resilience is my reason to keep going. Thank you for letting Daddy grieve out loud and still believe.

To my parents, Pamela and Tyrone Sr., and my brother, Tyrone II, brother-in-law Laud Okoh, sister-in-law Alicia Okoh, nephew Joseph Okoh, extended family and friends—your prayers held me up when I could no longer pray for myself. You taught me that spiritual inheritance is not just in what we teach but in how we survive together.

To the mothers, fathers, siblings, and friends who have lost children—I wrote this for you. I carry your names and your tears as sacred text. May these pages make space for your anger, your questions, and your still-beating love.

To my fellow chaplains, ministers, and theologians—you reminded me that sacred rage is not a threat to our faith but a witness to its depth. Thank you for your scholarship, your witness, and your refusal to let theology sanitize our grief.

To the communities and congregations who welcomed my story with reverence—you made it holy. Thank you for hearing my lament and not rushing me toward a resolution.

And finally, to the God who absorbs my fury without flinching, who sits in silence when I can't bear another promise, and who weeps beside me—I believe, even when I scream.

This book is for every soul who has ever said, "Take me instead," and lived to find a new question in the ashes.

Faith-Based Introduction

*"Tears are prayers too. They travel to God
when we cannot speak."*

—JEWISH PROVERB

Though grief manifests differently across religions, cultures, and traditions, one thread weaves them together—the sacred ache of love enduring loss. While exploring Jewish lament, Islamic *sabr*, and communal African mourning, I recognized myself in all of them. These are not distant rituals but sacred mirrors reflecting my own journey after losing Brooklyn. Grief is the universal language of hearts shattered by love too fierce to forget. This book is my bridge between theology and experience, between shared Scripture and a deeply personal pain.

Grief is not a sickness to cure. It is a landscape to live in, a vast and ever-changing terrain that defies our attempts to map it neatly. For those who have lost a child, grief is not an episode that passes; it is a permanent companion, a shadow that shifts with the light but never fully disappears. It is woven into every breath, every heartbeat, every memory, and every future dream that will never be realized. It becomes part of the framework of our lives, not as an unwelcome guest but as a testament to the depth of our love. We do not "heal" from this pain in the way the world expects.

Healing implies a return to a previous state of wholeness, but grief transforms us irrevocably. Instead, we learn how to live, breathe, and even love again—while carrying the unfillable hole left behind. We learn to coexist with our sorrow, to find moments of beauty amid the ache, to laugh without guilt, and to cry without shame. This is not the linear journey of "moving on" but the sacred, spiraling path of moving forward, carrying our grief as both burden and beacon. Within the Christian tradition, phrases like "have hope" and "trust God's plan" are often shared as comforts.

However, when standing amid the landscape of loss, such words can feel distant, their warmth elusive. Sincere hope does not seek to overshadow sorrow but to coexist with it, honoring the ache while whispering of resilience. It is within this tender tension that faith breathes—not as an antidote to doubt but as a companion to it, as capable of cradling protest as it is of uplifting praise. The Psalms lay bare this sacred paradox, weaving a tapestry rich with human emotion. Psalm 34:18 proclaims, "The LORD is near to the brokenhearted, and saves the crushed in spirit."

This is not a mere comforting phrase; it is a declaration of divine proximity in our most fragmented states. Brokenness, far from repelling God, becomes the very ground upon which God stands closest, affirming that our shattered-ness is not a void but a vessel of sacred encounter. Consider Ps 22, where the psalmist cries out, "My God, my God, why have you forsaken me? Why are you so far from saving me, so far from my cries of anguish?" (Ps 22:1). These words echo through the ages, even on the lips of Jesus as he hung on the cross. They validate the divulgence of our grief, the anguish that feels too heavy to bear.

Yet, within the same psalm, there is a shift: "You who fear the Lord, praise him! All you descendants of Jacob, honor him!" (verse 23). This oscillation between despair and praise reflects the complexity of grief—a sacred dance between lament and trust. In the Jewish tradition, lament is a recognized form of prayer.[1] The book

---

1. The Jewish practice of sitting shiva (the name for a period of mourning) lasts seven days after a loved one's burial. Mourners gather in their home while others visit, share stories, and offer comfort without forcing platitudes.

of Lamentations is a complete collection of poetic laments for the destruction of Jerusalem. It does not rush to resolution but dwells in the sorrow, offering space for grief to be fully expressed.

Lamentations 3:22–23 states, "Because of the Lord's great love we are not consumed, for his compassions never fail. They are new every morning; great is Your faithfulness." This passage does not negate the pain but offers a glimmer of hope amid the ruins. In Islam, *sabr*—sacred patience—is the thread that binds the shattered heart to God's mercy.[2] The Qur'an speaks to this in Surah Al-Baqarah 2:155–56: "And We will surely test you with something of fear and hunger and a loss of wealth and lives and fruits, but give good tidings to the patient, Who, when disaster strikes them, say, 'Indeed we belong to Allāh, and indeed to Him we will return.'"[3]

This acknowledgment of loss is not a dismissal but an integral part of faith. It recognizes the reality of suffering while anchoring the soul in divine remembrance. Across many African and Indigenous traditions, the grief of one is the grief of many—ancestral memory holds space for both loss and legacy.[4] Mourning becomes a communal act, a shared rite that honors the interconnectedness of lives. Rituals, songs, and stories create a tapestry of remembrance, ensuring that the departed are not forgotten. In these traditions, grief is not a solitary burden but a collective experience, woven into the community's composition.

Across faiths, grief is not denied; it is dignified. It is given space to exist without the pressure of resolution. And yet, too often

---

Mirrors are often covered, and meals are provided by the community, allowing space for grief without distraction.

2. The concept of sabr (the Islamic view of grief) in Islam goes beyond passive endurance. It calls for dignified patience grounded in remembrance of God (*dhikr*) and surrender to divine wisdom. Public lament is allowed, but harming oneself or questioning God's justice is discouraged. Grief is not faithlessness—it is an honest encounter with divine will.

3. From the Saheeh International translation of the Qur'an.

4. In many West African cultures, communal grieving rituals involve singing, drumming, storytelling, and dance—not to dismiss grief but to embody and express it. These practices affirm that the dead continue to live on through memory and action and that mourning is as much about connection as it is about loss.

in religious spaces, those of us shattered by the death of a child feel unseen. Too many sermons rush toward resurrection, skipping over the blood, the silence, the tomb. In their haste to offer comfort, they unintentionally dismiss the depth of our despair.

Too many prayers ask us to forgive, to accept, to praise—before we have even been allowed to scream. The sacredness of our pain is overlooked in the pursuit of theological neatness. *Sacred rage* is born from the refusal to sanitize grief. It is a love that did not die with them. It is the holy anger that says, "This is not how it was supposed to be—and yet, even now, God is here."

Sacred rage is not blasphemy; it is a form of worship, an acknowledgment of the weighty injustice of death and the enduring presence of love. It is the cry of the heart that refuses to be silenced, the demand for acknowledgment in a world that prefers neat narratives. This book is not a guide for how to "move on." It is a witness for how to move forward—carrying memory, sorrow, and sacred love in one trembling, triumphant body. It is an offering to those navigating the uncharted waters of grief, a companion for the journey that does not prescribe steps but stands in solidarity.

It acknowledges that grief is not linear, not a checklist to be completed, but an ever-evolving process. Some days are marked by fragile peace, others by waves of anguish that feel as fresh as the first moment of loss. Both are valid. Both are sacred. For the parent who cannot explain the weight they now carry, whose language has been shattered alongside their heart, this is a recognition of that unspeakable burden.

It is for the family who wants to support but cannot understand, struggling to find the right words when none exist. For the churches, mosques, temples, and chaplains who need better language for the unspeakable, who seek to create spaces where grief is honored, not hurried. For the counselors, teachers, and healers standing at the edges of sacred loss, bearing witness with compassionate presence. It is written from the trenches of grief—not from the polished pulpit but from the raw, messy ground where faith meets fury. Grief is not sanitized here; it is blunt, unfiltered, and real.

It is a testament to the coexistence of despair and hope, love and loss, sacredness and sorrow. Here, you will not be asked to be okay. You will be invited to be real—real with your pain, real with your rage, real with your love. Your rage is sacred. It speaks of love so fierce that it refuses to be diminished by death.

Your sorrow is sacred. It is the echo of a bond that transcends time and space. Your child's memory is sacred. It lives on in your heart, your stories, your tears, and your triumphs. And you—you who have survived the unimaginable—you are sacred, too. Your breath is a testament to resilience; your grief, a marker of great love.

"He heals the brokenhearted and binds up their wounds" (Ps 147:3). These words are not platitudes but promises, not meant to fix but to hold. They are the gentle reminder that in our most shattered moments, we are not abandoned. May this book be a small light for your sacred path. A flicker of hope in the darkness, a companion in the loneliness, a validation of your sacred rage and sorrow. May it honor your grief, not as a problem to solve but as a sacred journey to be witnessed and dignified.

Grief may change with time, but it does not disappear. It integrates into who we are, shaping our perspectives, our relationships, and our sense of self. It teaches us lessons we never asked to learn about the fragility of life, the depth of love, and the ways in which loss carves new spaces within us. Yet, within these hollowed spaces, unexpected growth can occur—resilience, empathy, and a profound connection to the suffering of others.

As we continue on this path, let us remember that grief is as unique as the love that preceded it. There is no right way to grieve, no timeline to follow, no expectations to meet. Your journey is your own, sacred in its authenticity. Share your story when you can, hold it close when you must. Allow others to walk beside you, even when they cannot fully understand.

May you find moments of peace amid the turbulence, glimpses of beauty within the pain, and the courage to carry your grief with the honor it deserves. You are not alone. You are seen. You are loved. Before sacred rage had a name, it lived inside me, unspoken. It began the day Brooklyn passed away and the world split open. What follows is not doctrine—it's testimony. An honest, trembling journey where faith limps, love screams, and grief becomes holy ground.

CHAPTER 1

The Day the World Broke

The wound is the place where the Light enters you.

—RUMI

The Scriptures say, "My God, my God, why have you forsaken me?" (Matt 27:46). These words, spoken by Jesus as he hung on the cross, held weight, revealing both his deep connection to humanity and the unapologetic nature of his suffering. This cry is a direct quotation from Ps 22—a psalm attributed to King David, which begins with an agonizing lament but transitions into trust, hope, and eventual praise. When Jesus uttered these words, he was not only expressing his own desolation but also anchoring his suffering in the sacred texts familiar to his listeners.

Psalm 22 begins with despair: "My God, my God, why have you forsaken me? Why are you so far from helping me, from the words of my groaning?" (Ps 22:1). It paints a vivid picture of abandonment, of feeling unheard and unseen. Yet, as the psalm progresses, it shifts toward a declaration of faith: "Yet you are holy, enthroned on the praises of Israel" (Ps 22:3). This juxtaposition of deep sorrow and unwavering faith mirrors the journey of grief itself—a path marked by both lament and longing for hope.

Jesus' cry was not one of faithlessness; rather, it was an honest expression of his humanity. Even in his divinity, he embraced the full spectrum of human emotion. His anguish validates our own. It tells us that grief and faith are not mutually exclusive. We can feel abandoned and still believe. We can scream into the void and still be held by God. Jesus' words on the cross sanctify our own cries of "Why?" and "Where are You?"—making space for grief within the sacred.

Consider, too, the cultural and religious context of Jesus' lament. In Jewish tradition, quoting the first line of a psalm often implied the entirety of the psalm. Those who heard Jesus' words would recall not only the anguish of Ps 42's beginning—"As a deer longs for flowing streams, so my soul longs for you, O God" (verse 1)—but also the deep yearning and hope embedded within it. By invoking this psalm, Jesus was connecting suffering to a broader narrative—a narrative that acknowledges grief while pointing toward the comforting presence of God.

This reflection reassures us theologically that grief is not an isolated experience but part of a sacred dialogue with God. It highlights that even in the depth of despair, there exists an undercurrent of hope and divine companionship, affirming that our sorrow is both seen and met with enduring grace.

In the depths of grief, it can feel as though God is distant, silent, or absent. This feeling is not new. The Bible is full of lamentations—unsophisticated, unfiltered expressions of sorrow, anger, and confusion. The book of Lamentations itself is a poetic cry of despair following the destruction of Jerusalem. The Psalms are filled with verses that question God's presence: "How long, O LORD? Will you forget me forever? How long will you hide your face from me?" (Ps 13:1). These sacred texts do not shy away from grief; they embrace it as part of the human experience.

When Jesus approached Jerusalem and foresaw its impending destruction, Jesus wept over the city, saying, "If you, even you, had only recognized on this day the things that make for peace!

But now they are hidden from your eyes" (Luke 19:41–42). Jesus knew what was to come yet did not withhold the depth of sorrow for the city's fate. These tears were not ceremonial; they were honest and authentic expressions of grief for the people and the injustices they would endure.

This sacred moment teaches that divine love is not indifferent or removed. Instead, it dwells among us, intimately connected with our sorrows and injustices. This echoes the role of ancestral grief in many African traditions, where the sorrow of loss is a communal burden, not a private wound. Death is mourned not with silence but with shared rituals that affirm the life and spirit of the deceased. Through the collective cry, the community declares, "This life mattered." In the context of grief, particularly the unbearable weight of losing a child—a grief that feels like an affront to justice itself—this narrative reminds us that *sacred rage* is not a betrayal of faith but an alignment with divine compassion. It is the heart's natural response to the rupture of life's fragile sanctity.

Sacred rage acknowledges the dissonance between the world as it is and as it ought to be. It does not seek to bypass grief but to sit with it, honor it, and name it. This rage, tempered by divine presence, becomes a testament to love's refusal to accept injustice as final. God weeps with us, not because of powerlessness but because of immense love that holds space for both grief and the hope of justice yet to come.

The cross itself is a testament to the coexistence of agony and hope. It is both the site of unimaginable suffering and the doorway to resurrection. Jesus' death was not sanitized or easy. It was brutal, public, and filled with anguish. And yet, within that suffering was the seed of redemption. The resurrection did not erase the pain of the crucifixion, but it reframed it within a larger story—a story where death is not the end.

This is the paradox of grief and faith. We do not need to choose between mourning and believing. The two can exist side by side. Faith does not eliminate pain; it provides a context for it. Let us pause and breathe together here, before we go on. Even the sacred texts take breaks between laments—so may we. In the ache, there is also an invitation to stillness. It reminds us that our suffering is seen, known, and honored by God. The Bible does not offer easy answers or quick fixes for grief. Instead, it offers presence—God's presence with us in our sorrow.

The apostle Paul wrote, "For we do not have a high priest who is unable to empathize with our weaknesses, but we have one who has been tempted in every way, just as we are—yet he did not sin" (Heb 4:15). Jesus' empathy is born from experience. He knows what it is to weep, to feel forsaken, to suffer deeply. This knowledge does not remove our pain, but it assures us that we are not alone in it.

When the world broke for Jesus on the cross, he did not suppress his anguish. He cried out. His vulnerability was sacred. In that moment, the curtain of the temple was torn in two (Matt 27:51), symbolizing that the barrier between God and humanity had been removed. Our pain, our grief, our "why" questions— none of these separate us from God. Instead, they are invitations to deeper connection.

The Scriptures provide insights into the aftermath of suffering. In Isa 61:3 it is written, ". . . to provide for those who mourn in Zion—to give them a garland instead of ashes, the oil of gladness instead of mourning, the mantle of praise instead of a faint spirit." This passage does not negate the depths of our grief or the sacred rage that may accompany it. Instead, it situates these powerful emotions within the transformative presence of God, highlighting a sacred transfiguration that transcends mere endurance. This divine exchange invites us into a reorientation of our spirit, woven through the enduring faithfulness and mystery of God's presence amid our sorrow.

The resurrection does not negate the cross; it gives it meaning. In the same way, growth does not erase grief; it reshapes it. Jesus' scars did not disappear after his resurrection. When he appeared to his disciples, he showed them his hands and his side (John 20:20). The marks of his suffering remained, not as symbols of defeat but as testimonies to his enduring love.

In your grief, you carry sacred scars—reminders of a love so unconditional that its loss has carved itself into your soul. These scars are not signs of brokenness beyond repair. They are evidence of a love that has touched you deeply, a love that continues to shape your story.

Grief is not easy nor the same. It is not orderly. It does not follow a schedule. It is wild, sacred, and deeply personal. The Psalms give us permission to lament. The cross gives us permission to cry out. The resurrection gives us hope that even in the darkest places, light can emerge.

Your grief is valid. Your pain is sacred. Your story is ongoing. As you navigate the "after," know that you are not alone. The Scriptures are filled with voices who have walked this path before you—voices that cry, question, rage, and hope. Join your voice with theirs. Let your lament be part of the sacred chorus. And remember, even in the silence, even in the darkness, you are held by a love that never let's go.

Key Reflection

- Grief and faith can coexist without contradiction.
- Jesus' lament invites us to bring our own sorrow into sacred space.
- Crying out is not the absence of faith—it is its fiercest expression

Chapter 1—The Day the World Broke

- What memories stand out most from the day your world changed?
- How do you feel when you think about that day? Sadness? Rage? Numbness? Something else?
- If you could say anything to yourself on the day your world broke, what would it be?
- Where, even in the smallest ways, have you seen traces of God's presence after that day?

CHAPTER 2

Sacred Rage: The Love That Refused to Die

Even the strong are broken by grief.

—ANCIENT SUMERIAN PROVERB

T here is a lie often whispered to grieving parents: "If you truly trusted God, you wouldn't be so angry." But the truth is this—*sacred rage is not a rejection of love. It is love refusing to die,* the fierce heartbeat that refuses to be silenced even when faced with the overwhelming void left by loss. When you lose a child, rage is not a failure of faith; it is the furious echo of all the hopes, dreams, and prayers that now have nowhere to go. It is the body's protest against a broken world, a rebellion against the notion that death has the final say, and the soul's scream declaring that the love shared, moments cherished, and life lost mattered.

In the Bible, we find the story of Job, a man whose faith was severely tested through unimaginable loss. Job tore his robe, shaved his head, and fell to the ground—not in quiet acceptance but in unflinching grief and protest. This act of tearing one's robe and shaving the head was a traditional expression of deep mourning in ancient Near Eastern cultures, symbolizing an outward manifestation of the internal devastation. His actions were not mere rituals; they embodied deep, uncontainable sorrow surging through him. In Job 3:11, he cried out, "Why did I not die at birth, come forth from the womb and expire?" These words are not of a man devoid of faith but of one intimately connected with God, pouring cut his heart in agony.

Job's rage was not faithlessness but intimacy—an unwillingness to pretend before God. It was the courage to stand naked in grief, baring the full weight of his sorrow without masking it with platitudes or shallow comfort. Sacred rage does not deny God—it demands that God meet us here, where the world went wrong. Like Job, like Jesus in Gethsemane, we ask, plead, shout. We rage because we love. His dialogues with God throughout the book of Job are unfiltered, and direct, challenging the simplistic theology of his friends who insisted that suffering was always a result of sin. Job's sacred rage opens a space where grief and faith coexist, where one's relationship with God is not weakened by anguish but deepened through honesty.

Sacred rage proclaims, "*This should not have happened. My child's life mattered too much to be brushed aside.*" I refuse to shrink my sorrow to make others comfortable. I refuse to betray my love by pretending the pain is smaller than it is. In sacred rage, we meet the God who tore the temple veil, breaking barriers between God and human, the sacred and the profane. The tearing of the temple veil at the moment of Jesus' death (Matt 27:51) symbolizes the removal of the separation between God and humanity, signifying that in our deepest despair, we are never alone.

We encounter the Christ who overturned tables in the temple courts (John 2:13–16), consumed by righteous anger at corruption and injustice within sacred spaces. This wasn't mere anger. It was sacred protest—love acting against corruption, grief crying out against injustice. Jesus' actions weren't impulsive rage but deeply purposeful, revealing a divine love that does not stay silent in the face of harm. His protest reclaims the sacred, showing us that anger aligned with love can be an instrument of justice.

In Jewish tradition, the temple veil separated the Holy of Holies—the most sacred space—from the people. When Jesus died, the veil tore (Matt 27:51), symbolizing that no pain, no grief, no rage separates us from God. The Divine steps into our lowness. This was not a passive Savior but one who felt deeply, loved fiercely, and acted boldly. Jesus' anger was not a loss of control but an embodiment of divine justice and sacred passion, revealing that emotions, even intense ones, have a place in the life of faith. And yet, even here, a flicker of peace remains—peace not as the absence of emotion but as the sacred space where rage and love both have room to breathe. His actions challenge the notion that spirituality requires detachment from strong feelings. Instead, they affirm that sacred rage reflects love and a commitment to truth.

Consider the Spirit who groans with us when words fail, offering comfort not through empty phrases but through presence, understanding, and shared grief. Romans 8:26 tells us, "Likewise the Spirit helps us in our weakness, . . . that very Spirit intercedes with groanings too deep for words." This powerful imagery speaks to the depth of divine empathy, where even when we cannot articulate our pain, God's Spirit resonates with our suffering. It is a reminder that sacred rage and grief are not obstacles to divine connection but conduits through which God's presence becomes most palpable.

Sacred rage is the fire that burns away shallow platitudes, rejecting the notion that grief must be considerable or that faith requires silence in pain. It is the holy inferno consuming the rubble of pretense, clearing space for something honest, sacred, fierce, and real to rise in its place. It acknowledges that grief is a never-ending journey, moving forward does not mean forgetting, and love does not expire with life.

Consider the story of Jacob wrestling with God in Gen 32:22–32. Jacob's struggle was both physical and spiritual, a nightlong battle that left him wounded but transformed. He refused to let go until he received a blessing, embodying the tenacity of sacred rage.

This narrative teaches us that wrestling with God is not an act of defiance but an expression of deep faith—a refusal to settle for easy answers when faced with life's most unfathomable questions.

Sacred rage does not indicate turning against God; instead, it means standing in the sacred place where honesty and divinity collide. It signifies wrestling with God, much like Jacob did, refusing to let go until finding some semblance of blessing—or at least understanding. It declares that your pain is too significant to be hidden, deserving full acknowledgment in its rusticity. Sacred rage bridges the chasm between human suffering and divine empathy, affirming that even in our deepest agony, we are seen, heard, and held. Before we continue, take a moment. What if your grief doesn't need resolution right now? What if it only needs to be heard, honored, and held?

In the book of Job, we encounter ambiguous expressions of sacred rage woven through the narrative of suffering and loss. Job 3:11 cries out, "Why did I not die at birth, come forth from the womb and expire?"—a piercing lament that echoes the anguish of one grappling with complex forms of grief and the seeming absence of divine justice. This passage does not shy away from the crassness of despair but moves through it, creating space for both sorrow and the search for meaning. Job's courage to voice such unfiltered anguish within sacred Scripture affirms our own struggles with pain and protest.

Sacred rage, as seen in Job's lament, is not an affront to God but an authentic engagement with the reality of suffering. It acknowledges that grief, especially in the face of unimaginable loss like the death of children, often feels like an injustice—an unraveling of the moral understanding we expect to hold firm. Yet, within this sacred text, there is a theological reassurance: the divine presence is not contingent upon our silence or stoicism in suffering. Instead, God listens, holds space, and even honors our cries.

Job's journey reveals that sacred rage is part of a dynamic relationship with God, where questioning and grieving are met not with condemnation but with an expansive, enduring presence. This understanding brings comfort in the face of injustice,

9

affirming that our grief and protests are not signs of faith's weakness but expressions of its depth.

Similarly, the book of Lamentations is a poetic outpouring of grief over the destruction of Jerusalem. Its verses are filled with sorrow, anger, and questions directed at God. Yet, amid the devastation, there is an acknowledgment of God's enduring presence: "Because of the LORD's great love, we are not consumed, for his compassions never fail" (Lam 3:22). This tension between despair and hope reflects the complex nature of sacred rage—a space where deep sorrow and unwavering faith coexist.

Even Jesus, in the garden of Gethsemane, exemplifies sacred rage and grief. In Matt 26:39, he falls to the ground, praying, "My Father, if it is possible, may this cup be taken from me. Yet not as I will, but as you will." His anguish was so intense that Luke 22:44 describes his sweat as "like drops of blood falling to the ground." Jesus' vulnerability in this moment reveals that sacred rage and sorrow are integral to the human experience, even for the Son of God.

Sacred rage is not about losing faith but about engaging with it on the most authentic level. It challenges us to confront the injustices and losses in our lives without diminishing their impact. It invites us to hold our pain in the light of divine presence, trusting that God can handle our most difficult emotions.

In conclusion, sacred rage is a testament to the depth of our love and the intensity of our grief. It is an honest, unfiltered response to the brokenness of the world, a cry that echoes through the Scriptures and resonates with the heart of God. It teaches us that faith is not the absence of struggle but the courage to engage with it fully. Sacred rage is where we meet God—not in the polished platitudes of comfort but in the turbulent, sacred spaces of our deepest pain.

Key Reflection

- Grief and faith can coexist without contradiction.
- Jesus' lament invites us to bring our own sorrow into sacred space.
- Crying out is not the absence of faith—it is its fiercest expression.

Chapter 2—Sacred Rage: The Love That Refused to Die

Before you begin, take a deep breath. Inhale slowly, hold for four seconds, and exhale gently. Let your breath remind you that you are still here. Still surviving. Still sacred.

- Whether or not you believe in God today, what would it look like to trust love again—even if it's fierce, even if it's angry?
- What angers you most about your loss?
- Have you ever been made to feel ashamed of your anger? By yourself? By others?
- What would it feel like to believe that your rage is seen —and even held—by the sacred?
- If God feels far, what language or presence do you wish could hold your pain?
- What tables would you turn over if you could, in honor of your child's life?

CHAPTER 3

Their Name: A Name Written in Eternity

To live in hearts we leave behind is not to die.

—THOMAS CAMPBELL

Some names are not just spoken; they are sung into the soul. Our Brooklyn—a name that carries weight, light, and life, even when spoken through tears. It is more than letters; it is an anthem, a melody that echoes in hearts where grief and memory intertwine. Our loved one's name does not vanish with death but is stitched into the construction of eternity. It reverberates, a testament to the enduring impact of her life.

The day our loved one left this world marked not just sorrow but a seismic shift in the hearts of those who loved her. Though the sky appeared the same and the sun shone as usual, the world tilted slightly, forever altered. The air grew heavier, woven with threads of loss and undying love. Heaven bore witness to a love so fierce that even death could not silence it. Her absence created a sacred space filled with memories and heartfelt grief.

Grief is not forgetting; it is remembering with sacred rage, broken prayers, and holy defiance. It means standing at the edge of loss and declaring, "Her life mattered. Her light still burns." To grieve Brooklyn is to honor her existence, to proclaim that her story endures despite her absence. Grief is a living monument built from memories, laughter, and tears. It reflects boundless love, not weakness.

Memories come like waves—her laughter, her touch, and her dreams yet unlived. They arrive unexpectedly: the echo of her voice in a quiet room, a scent that reminds you of her, or sunlight filtering through trees on a familiar day. Sometimes silence is heavy, louder than any sound, filled with her absence. Yet in both the flood of memories and the drought of silence, Brooklyn's name is not erased. It lingers in hearts, whispered by angels and etched into the soul.

In Ps 56:8, the psalmist says, "You have kept count of my tossings; put my tears in your bottle. Are they not in your record?" This verse is a reminder of God's intimate awareness of our suffering. The imagery of God collecting our tears in a bottle speaks to his deep compassion and care for each moment of our grief. It reflects a divine attentiveness that ensures none of our sorrows are unnoticed. The reference to our tears being recorded in God's book assures us that every pain, every loss, and every struggle is acknowledged in the heavenly realm.

The cultural context of this verse adds even more depth. In ancient times, tear bottles were used during periods of mourning to collect tears as tangible expressions of grief. These small, delicate vessels were often kept as reminders of love and loss, symbolizing the emotional journey of those left behind. The psalmist draws from this imagery to convey that God himself acts as the ultimate keeper of our sorrows. He does not dismiss or overlook our pain; instead, he holds it sacred and dear. This verse reassures us that their memory is not forgotten in the divine realm. Each tear shed in her absence is sacred and cherished. Our grief is acknowledged and tenderly held by God.

This connection between human sorrow and divine compassion is echoed in other Scriptures as well. In Rev 21:4, we are comforted with the promise, "He will wipe every tear from their eyes. Death will be no more; mourning and crying and pain will be no more, for the first things have passed away." This verse speaks to the ultimate hope that grief will not be our final story. The pain we feel now is temporary compared to the eternal comfort that awaits us. The imagery of God personally wiping away tears illustrates his tender care and intimate involvement in our moving forward. It assures us that the brokenness of this world will one day be replaced with perfect peace and unending joy.

Another powerful Scripture is found in Matt 5:4: "Blessed are those who mourn, for they shall be comforted." This beatitude from Jesus' Sermon on the Mount turns the world's understanding of grief upside down. It suggests that mourning is not a sign of weakness but a pathway to divine comfort. It acknowledges the pain of loss while simultaneously promising that God's presence will meet us in that pain. In the original Greek, the word for "comforted" (*parakaleo*) conveys the idea of someone coming alongside to offer support and encouragement. It paints a picture of God drawing near to the brokenhearted, providing solace and strength in our most vulnerable moments.

Psalm 147:3 reminds us of this comforting truth: "[God] heals the brokenhearted, and binds up their wounds." The closeness of God during times of grief isn't just a hopeful idea—it's an abstruse reality. The Divine doesn't remain distant; instead, this sacred presence steps right into our sorrow, offering solace and renewal as the guiding force to help us move forward. This closeness isn't dependent on our own strength or resilience. It's a gift freely given, a testament to unwavering love and boundless compassion.

Deuteronomy 31:6 offers further reassurance: "Be strong and courageous. Do not be afraid or terrified because of them, for the LORD your God goes with you; [God] will never leave you nor forsake you." This verse speaks directly to the heart of those grappling with loss. It acknowledges the fear and dismay that often accompany grief while simultaneously providing a promise of divine support. The Divine's strength is made perfect in our weakness, and sacred help is ever-present in times of trouble.

Psalm 136:26 beautifully encapsulates the enduring nature of God's love: "Give thanks to the God of heaven, for his steadfast love endures forever." This passage serves as a powerful reminder that not even the changes and challenges of life can sever the bond of divine love. Their presence in our lives may have shifted, but the love that connects us to them—and to God—remains unbroken.

Their legacy is woven into the present, inspiring courage, shaping lives, and nurturing hearts. We honor her not by pretending to be unbroken but by carrying her memory with sacred fire and trembling hands. *We rage because we loved her deeply,* and we hope because she remains beloved. Moving forward doesn't mean leaving her behind; it means carrying her with us, step by step. Every act of kindness and love continues her story.

Her presence is found in quiet moments—the pause before a prayer, the flicker of a candle, or a heartbeat quickened by memory. She lives in the courage to smile through tears and the strength to face another day. Grief demands resilience, and through it, Brooklyn's light shines undiminished. Her memory inspires us to live fully and love fiercely. She is not forgotten; her essence endures within us.

To speak their name is to conjure all they were: vibrant, beloved, irreplaceable. Acknowledging their name honors both the depth of loss and the magnitude of enduring love. Their story is not closed; it continues in the hearts they touched. Their laughter echoes in the joy of those who remember them. Their dreams inspire others to live boldly, dream fearlessly, and love passionately.

Grief is a journey, not a destination, shaping us and allowing growth even amid loss. They walk with us—not as a shadow of the past but as a beacon of what continues to be. Their name calls us to live a life that honors their spirit, balancing sorrow with joy. We create beauty from broken hearts, holding their legacy close. Their story is defined by love that endures, not by absence.

As we navigate grief's waves, we find solace in knowing Brooklyn is not forgotten. Her name is etched into our very being, a testament to a life that mattered deeply. The love we hold for her is sacred, a flame that darkness cannot extinguish. Her light still burns in every act of remembrance and every heartbeat that carries her forward. Her story lives on, sung in the souls that carry her name—Brooklyn—a name stitched into the foundation of eternity.

Key Reflection

- Grief and faith can coexist without contradiction.

- Jesus' lament invites us to bring our own sorrow into sacred space.

- Crying out is not the absence of faith—it is its fiercest expression.

Chapter 3—Their Name: A Name Written in Eternity

> *Sit quietly for a moment. Place your hand on your heart.*
> *Say their name aloud if you feel safe to do so.*

- If you do not believe in a divine afterlife, what does it mean to let their legacy live through you? What is love's role in remembrance?

- What are the moments when your child's memory feels closest to you?

- How has your love for them changed, deepened, or grown even after their passing?

- What sacred rituals, prayers, or traditions might you create to honor their ongoing presence in your life?

- How has your child's memory shaped your purpose or redefined what matters most in your life?

- Write a letter to your child, telling them how you carry their love forward.

CHAPTER 4

When Faith Feels like a Lie

Even the darkness will not be dark to You; the night will
shine like the day, for darkness is as light to You.

—PSALM 139:12

T he exploration of sacred grief and faith in the face of loss, as presented in the original text, provides a specific foundation rooted in Scripture. To delve deeper, we will examine the biblical context, incorporate additional scriptural narratives, and contemplate the theological implications of suffering and divine presence.

The Universality of Grief in Scripture

From Genesis to Revelation, the Bible is unflinching in its portrayal of human suffering. This perspective of unvarnished honesty is a testament to the sacredness of every human emotion, including grief, anger, and doubt.

Hannah's Silent Lament (1 Sam 1:9–18)

Consider Hannah, who wept bitterly before the Lord because of her barrenness. Her silent prayers were so intense that Eli, the priest, mistook her for being drunk. Hannah's story illustrates that grief can be silent, hidden beneath the surface, yet heard by God. Her anguish led to a heartfelt prayer, one that eventually resulted in the birth of Samuel. However, the significance lies not in the outcome but in the fact that her pain was seen, and her silent lament acknowledged by God.

Jeremiah: The Weeping Prophet

Jeremiah, known as the "weeping prophet," provides another powerful example. His entire ministry was marked by sorrow as he witnessed the fall of Jerusalem and the suffering of his people. In Lamentations and throughout his prophecies, Jeremiah's unbridled expressions of grief are recorded without censorship. He questioned, mourned, and even accused God of deception (Jer 20:7), yet his relationship with God remained intact. This complex dynamic underscores that faith is not about perfect piety but about honest engagement with God.

The Garden of Gethsemane: Jesus' Agony (Matt 26:36–46)

In the garden of Gethsemane, Jesus' prayer before his arrest reveals the depth of his human anguish. He was "sorrowful and troubled," even to the point of sweating "like drops of blood" (Luke 22:44). Jesus prayed, "My Father, if it is possible, let this cup pass from me. Yet not as I will, but as you will" (Matt 26:39). This moment highlights that even the Son of God wrestled with the weight of impending suffering. His prayer mirrors the cries of countless believers, torn between the desire for relief and the struggle to submit to God's will.

The Apostle Paul: Strength in Weakness
(2 Cor 12:7–10)

Paul's "thorn in the flesh"—an affliction he pleaded with God to remove—remained despite his fervent prayers. God's response, "My grace is sufficient for you, for my power is made perfect in weakness" (2 Cor 12:9), reveals a divine paradox. Sometimes, God's answer is not deliverance but the provision of grace to endure. Paul's acceptance of this truth transformed his perspective on suffering: "For whenever I am weak, then I am strong" (2 Cor 12:10). This statement reflects the countercultural truth that vulnerability is not a failure of faith but a space where God's strength is most evident.

The Theology of Lament

Lament is not merely an expression of sorrow; it is a sacred act—an honest articulation of love interrupted. This truth echoes across faith traditions. In Buddhism, grief is not a detour from the path but part of the path itself.[1] It serves as a teacher, inviting us into deeper awareness of impermanence (*anicca*) and compassion (*karuṇā*). In Hinduism, rituals like *shraddha* honor ancestors through offerings and remembrance, affirming that the soul continues its journey and remains tethered to the family through acts of devotion.[2] Within the Hebrew Scriptures, lament acknowledges divine sovereignty not by masking pain but by expressing it fully. The psalms of lament follow a rhythm: grief voiced aloud, a plea for presence or relief, and sometimes a fragile declaration of trust. Yet not all laments end in praise—Psalm 88, for example, leaves the cry unresolved, reminding us that spiritual life makes room for the unanswered. Let us breathe there too—in the mystery, in the silence, in the spaces where even sacred language pauses.

---

1. Lion's Roar, "How Buddhism Helps."
2. Editors of Encyclopedia Britannica, "Shraddha."

Biblical Characters Who Wrestled with God

Moses: After leading the Israelites out of Egypt, Moses faced constant complaints and rebellion. In Num 11:11–15, he cried out to God in frustration, even asking for death. God's response was not to chastise Moses but to provide help by appointing elders to share the burden.

Habakkuk: The prophet boldly questioned God's justice, asking, "Why do you make me look at injustice? Why do you tolerate wrongdoing?" (Hab 1:3). God's response was complex, affirming that divine plans often operate beyond human understanding. Yet, Habakkuk's dialogue with God ended with a declaration of faith: "Yet I will rejoice in the LORD, I will be joyful in God my Savior" (Hab 3:18).

Mary and Martha: In John 11, when their brother Lazarus died, both sisters confronted Jesus with the same words: "Lord, if you had been here, my brother would not have died" (verses 21 and 32). Jesus' response was deeply personal—he wept with them, sharing in their grief, before performing the miracle of resurrection. This narrative underscores that even when God plans to bring life from death, he first sits with us in our mourning.

The Role of Community in Grief

Biblical grief is often communal. In the Old Testament, mourning was a shared ritual involving sackcloth, ashes, and public lamentation. The book of Job illustrates both the potential and the pitfalls of community in grief. Job's friends initially did the right thing: "They sat on the ground with him for seven days and seven nights. No one said a word to him because they saw how great his suffering was" (Job 2:13).

Community can be both balm and blade in grief. Friends mean well, but sometimes their words become walls—"God needed another angel," "everything happens for a reason." These platitudes don't heal; they hush. What grieving parents need is not answers but presence. The ministry of sitting in silence, like Job's friends before they started explaining, is far holier than any sermon. Their silent presence was a powerful act of solidarity. However, their later attempts to explain Job's suffering with theological platitudes caused more harm than good.

The Book of Revelation: Hope amid Suffering

Revelation, often associated with apocalyptic imagery, is a book of hope written to persecuted believers. Its vivid depictions of struggle and judgment are accompanied by promises of restoration: "He will wipe every tear from their eyes. Death will be no more; mourning and crying and pain will be no more" (Rev 21:4). This vision does not dismiss current suffering but places it within the context of God's redemptive plan.

Practical Reflections on Faith and Suffering

Permission to Lament: Recognize that lamenting is a valid spiritual practice. You do not need to sanitize your prayers. God invites your honesty.

Sacred Silence: Sometimes, the most faithful response is to sit in silence, acknowledging the mystery of suffering without rushing to explain it.

Community Support: Be present for those who grieve without offering quick fixes. Your presence is often more powerful than words.

The Power of Ritual: Engage in rituals that honor loss, such as lighting candles, writing prayers, or creating memorial spaces.

Continual Dialogue with God: Keep the conversation with God open, even when it feels one-sided. The act of reaching out is itself an act of faith.

Conclusion

The Scriptures are filled with stories of people who brought their whole selves—grief, doubt, anger, and hope—before God. Their experiences remind us that faith is not about having all the answers but about holding onto God even when our world falls apart. Your sacred rage, your lament, your broken prayers—they are not obstacles to faith but expressions of it. God is not distant from your pain. And if you're tired, let that be holy too. There's no need to rush toward hope. Rest is sacred. So is the pause between sobs. In fact, the biblical narrative reveals a God who enters into human suffering, who weeps, who listens, and who redeems. In the end, faith is not about the absence of struggle but the presence of God in the midst of it.

Key Reflection

- Grief and faith can coexist without contradiction.
- Jesus' lament invites us to bring our own sorrow into sacred space.
- Crying out is not the absence of faith—it is its fiercest expression.

Chapter 4—When Faith Feels like a Lie

- Have you ever felt abandoned by God during your grief?
- What words or phrases meant to "comfort" you actually made the pain feel worse?
- What honest prayer would you pray today if you believed God could handle your anger?
- How has your understanding of faith changed since your loss?

CHAPTER 5

Learning to Breathe Again: Tiny Acts of Survival

Breathe in, breathe out. This is the rhythm of survival.

—ANCIENT BUDDHIST PROVERB

G rief doesn't always manifest as a dramatic breakdown with floods of tears and outward expressions that are easily recognized. Sometimes, it's quiet and invisible, yet it weighs just as heavily as visible agony. It can look like brushing your teeth when you don't want to, each motion feeling like an insurmountable task. The mundane becomes monumental, a simple act transformed into a struggle against the gravity of loss. Surviving grief often starts with these small, unnoticed victories.

Putting on shoes just to step outside can be another battle against grief. It's not for a grand occasion but simply to feel the ground beneath your feet and face a world that feels foreign without your loved one. Each lace tied and every step taken is a defiant act against the weight of sorrow. Similarly, replying to a plain text message can feel overwhelming, yet it maintains the fragile thread of connection to the world outside your grief. These tiny actions, while insignificant, are the very stitches holding your spirit together.

After an unimaginable loss, survival is built on these small, almost invisible acts. Drink water. Write your child's name in a journal. Sit outside and let the sun touch your skin. These are not insignificant things. These are prayers in motion. Sacred survival looks like stretching, crying in the shower, breathing through the ache. Celebrate the small wins.

They may not make headlines or draw applause, but they highlight quiet courage and resilience. Getting out of bed, opening a window, feeding yourself, and folding laundry are daily rituals that signify a heart learning to beat again in an emptier world. Just breathing can feel like an act of rebellion against overwhelming sorrow. It's not about thriving but surviving—one breath, one moment at a time.

Breathing through the first morning without your child feels like facing an indifferent world while carrying an unbearable void. The sun rises as if nothing has changed, yet everything has—and still, you breathe. Holidays lose their warmth, but you continue breathing through songs and traditions that now echo with absence. The awkward glances and silences from others add layers of loneliness, but you persevere, holding onto fragile connections. Survivor's guilt weighs heavily, yet you breathe—not because you have answers but because it's all you can do.

In Ezek 37, God brings the prophet to a valley of dry bones, asking, "Can these bones live?" Ezekiel responds, "Sovereign Lord, you alone know" (verse 3), an honest truth mirrored in grief. This passage offers insight into the nature of restoration and hope amid insurmountable despair. The valley of dry bones symbolizes the depth of desolation and loss, where life appears completely absent. Yet, God's question to Ezekiel challenges the notion of finality in death and loss. It invites us to consider that even in our deepest grief, there is the potential for renewal.

The act of prophesying to the bones, as commanded by God, represents speaking life into what seems lifeless. In grief, tiny acts of survival become sacred: getting out of bed defies despair, laughing even briefly signals life amid darkness, and saying your child's name aloud preserves their memory. These small gestures are echoes of Ezekiel's prophecy—declarations that life persists even when enveloped in sorrow. Allowing yourself to feel joy without guilt is a bold statement that grief and joy can coexist. Each breath, each step forward, is not a betrayal but a testimony to the life and love you carry within you.

Isaiah 41:10 says, "Do not fear, for I am with you; do not be dismayed, for I am your God. I will strengthen you and help you; I will uphold you with my righteous right hand." This verse reassures us that in our most fragile moments, when grief feels like an insurmountable weight, God's presence is nearest. The broken heart is not disqualified from divine attention; rather, it is tenderly held. This closeness does not necessarily remove the pain but provides a sustaining grace that allows us to endure.

In the story of Job, we see another biblical exploration of grief and suffering. Job loses his wealth, health, and family, and his friends offer hollow explanations, trying to rationalize his pain. However, God does not condemn Job's honest lament and questioning. Instead, God engages with Job, not with clear answers but with a reminder of his vastness and presence. This narrative reinforces that grief does not need to be organized or theologically neat; it can be bare, messy, and filled with unanswered questions yet still held within God's compassionate gaze.

You're not moving on; you're carrying your loved one forward—one trembling breath at a time. Grief doesn't follow a linear path with a clear destination; it's a landscape navigated step-by-step, often with setbacks. There's no divine stopwatch timing your progress, and that's okay. God promises, "I will cause breath to enter you, and you shall live" (Ezek 37:5)—a promise of support, not a demand for quick recovery. Adjustments, alterations, are messy and unpredictable, but even the smallest acts of survival are sacred.

In Isa 61:3, we find the promise "to provide for those who mourn in Zion—to give them a garland instead of ashes, the oil of gladness instead of mourning, the mantle of praise instead of a faint spirit." This passage acknowledges the reality of mourning and despair but also speaks of transformation. It's not about erasing grief but about the possibility of beauty emerging from the ashes of sorrow. The "oil of joy" does not negate the mourning; it coexists with it, just as praise can flow from hearts still acquainted with despair.

Consider the lament psalms, such as Ps 13, where David cries out, "How long, O LORD? Will you forget me forever?" (verse 1). These words reflect the depths of despair and the feeling of divine absence. Yet, even within these lamentations, there's often a pivot—a remembrance of God's past faithfulness, a fragile thread of hope woven through the darkness. This duality holds space for both the pain of unanswered questions and the flicker of enduring faith.

You don't have to rebuild your life all at once or find meaning in your loss immediately, if ever. Some days, just breathing is enough; existing is enough. Simple actions like waking up, getting dressed, or making coffee become sacred acts of survival. Every breath, step, tear, and smile you manage to share is proof of resilience and the enduring power of love. Grief is not a weakness; it's a testament to the depth of your love.

Psalm 34:18 declares, "The LORD is near to the brokenhearted, and saves the crushed in spirit." This verse can offer comfort, especially to those who find themselves unable to articulate the depth of their sorrow. Even when words fail, our pain is not lost to God. The Divine's nearness assures us that our grief is both seen and understood.

In the theological context, this passage speaks to the deep connection between human suffering and the presence of God. It acknowledges that grief is not an isolated experience but one enveloped by God's attentive compassion. Grief, in its intemperateness, can stir sacred rage—a righteous, deeply felt response to loss, injustice, or deep pain. This sacred rage is not a divergence from faith but an integral part of the spiritual journey, reflecting a heart that deeply values what has been lost.

Rather than focusing solely on concepts like healing or restoration, this verse invites us into an experience of alignment—with God's presence in our suffering, with the truth of our emotions, and with the sacred acknowledgment that our deepest pains are valid and held within the vastness of divine understanding. In this sacred space, grief and sacred rage are not obstacles but pathways, guiding us closer to the heart of God, where every tear is noticed and every anguished cry is honored.

If all you can do today is breathe, that's enough. Sitting with your grief without rushing to "fix" it is perfectly okay. There's no timeline or expiration date for sorrow—it's a unique, sacred journey. Even in silence and darkness, you are not alone; God's presence whispers, "I will cause breath to enter you, and you shall live." For today, just breathe, and tomorrow, we'll see—but for now, breathing is enough.

Philippians 4:7 speaks of "the peace of God, which transcends all understanding, [that] will guard your hearts and your minds in Christ Jesus." This peace is not contingent upon our circumstances aligning with our desires. It's a peace that exists even when everything around us is in turmoil—a peace that guards, not just comforts. It doesn't demand that we stop grieving but holds us securely within our grief.

At the core of grief lies a sacred journey, not marked by grandiose gestures but by small, courageous acts of survival: rising from bed, acknowledging your pain, and uttering their name aloud. These are holy acts. Scripture doesn't offer a formula to erase suffering but instead presents a sacred tapestry—threads of lament, protest, divine presence, and unwavering hope woven through our deepest sorrows. From Job's silent anguish and self-scraping wounds to the psalmist's anguished cry, "How long, O LORD?" and Jesus' gasping, "My God, my God, why have you forsaken me?" we are reminded that grieving is not a rejection of faith. Grief and faith can coexist without contradiction.

In fact, grief may be one of the most faithful acts we ever undertake, as it speaks truthfully about love and loss in a world that often demands silence. We witness this in the vision of the dry bones in Ezekiel. The Spirit doesn't shame the scattered bones. Instead, God breathes into them and declares, "I will give you breath, and you shall live." Not because they were prepared or whole, but because God meets us in our fragmentation and calls life forth anyway.

The same is true for you. You are not asked to remain unshaken or rush toward joy. You are simply invited to be present—to the ache, to the breath, to the sacred pause between what was and what will be. In the end, the promise is not perfection but presence. Not answers, but companionship. Even now, even here, you are not alone.

Key Reflection

- Grief and faith can coexist without contradiction.

- Jesus' lament invites us to bring our own sorrow into sacred space.

- Crying out is not the absence of faith—it is its fiercest expression.

Chapter 5—Learning to Breathe Again: Tiny Acts of Survival

Pause and give yourself credit for being here.
For breathing. For showing up to the page.

- What does surviving mean for you today? How does your breath carry the memory of love forward, even when your strength feels small?

- What are the small acts of survival you've managed that others might not even notice?

- What tiny victories have you experienced since your loss, even if they seemed insignificant at the time?

- What parts of your identity have changed through surviving this loss? How do you see yourself now?

- How do you talk to yourself on the hard days—are you kind, patient, harsh?
- What does it mean to you to think of survival itself as sacred?

CHAPTER 6

Memory Is a Holy Place

Those we love and lose are always connected by heartstrings into infinity.

—TERRI GUILLEMETS

W hen the world moves on, memory holds the line. It stands unwavering, a sentinel guarding the echoes of laughter, the whispers of stories, and the quiet moments that once filled spaces with life. Memory is not a trap; it is not a failure to heal. Rather, it is a sacred archive, a testament to the depth of love and the resilience of the human spirit. Memory is a holy place—a temple where the heart seeks solace, where grief and love coexist in an intricate dance.

Each remembered laugh, each whispered story, each birthday celebrated in silence—these are not signs that you are stuck. They are signs that love outlives death. Love doesn't dissipate with absence; it transforms, anchoring itself in the sacred relics of memory. The world may be eager to "move on," but parents who have buried a child know: we don't move on. We carry forward. We build altars in the ruins.

We sit with the memories, light candles for the birthdays that never stop mattering, and speak the names the world is uncomfortable hearing. These rituals are not an inability to let go—they are acts of defiance against the erasure of a life deeply cherished. Communal memory ceremonies—like lighting candles together, sharing favorite stories of our loved ones, or simply saying their name—have become sacred acts of resistance. Resistance to forgetting. Resistance to being told to move on. In Deuteronomy, God commands the Israelites: "Remember the whole way that the LORD your God has led you" (Deut 8:2). This call to remembrance is an integral part of faith. Memory is part of faith.

Contextually, Deut 8:2 reflects a pivotal moment for the Israelites. Having wandered the wilderness for forty years, they were on the cusp of entering the promised land. God's directive to "remember the whole way" was not a mere historical recollection but a reflective spiritual exercise. It was a call to reflect on the trials, the divine provisions of manna, the lessons in humility, and the unwavering faithfulness of God. Their memories were more than stories; they were spiritual signposts, reminding them of God's presence in their journey—both in times of abundance and in seasons of scarcity.

This reflection invites us to consider how memory functions similarly in our lives. Just as the Israelites were guided by the hand of God through trials and triumphs, our personal stories are etched with moments of divine presence. In acknowledging this, we honor both the hardships and the blessings, recognizing that every part of our journey holds sacred value.

To remember is to honor. To remember is to declare that love was real—and is still real. It is to acknowledge that the footprints left on your heart are enduring, etched into the very essence of who you are. Grief sanctifies memory. It transforms ordinary moments into sacred ground, turning the last smile, the last touch, the last bedtime story into an altar.

These memories are more than recollections; they are spiritual anchors, connecting the temporal with the eternal. Consider the Israelites' festivals, such as Passover—a ritual rooted in remembrance. Each year, families recount the story of liberation from Egypt, reinforcing faith through storytelling, symbols, and customs. This act of remembering is not just about the past; it shapes identity, community, and hope for the future.

Memory also wounds. It can be an uninvited guest, breaking you open in the grocery store aisle when you see their favorite snack. It can gut you during a song you didn't realize would trigger a tidal wave of emotion. It can ambush you on anniversaries no one else remembers but you. These experiences are not weaknesses—they are the heart's natural response to an irreplaceable loss. And yet, memory is a holy rebellion. It refuses to let the world sanitize your grief or erase your child. Each time you tell their story, each time you remember their light, you are proclaiming, "This life mattered. Still matters. Will always matter."

You do not remember because you are weak. You remember because love demands to be remembered. Love is insistent, relentless in its desire to honor and preserve. It refuses to be silenced, echoing through the chambers of the heart, a testament to bonds that defy mortality. God remembers, too, as written in Isa 49:15–16: "Can a woman forget her nursing child, or show no compassion for the child of her womb? Even these may forget, yet I will not forget you. See, I have inscribed you on the palms of my hands; your walls are continually before me."

Isaiah's words were delivered to the Israelites during their exile in Babylon—a period marked by displacement, despair, and a sense of abandonment. Yet, through the prophet, God offers an image of divine remembrance so intimate and enduring that even a mother's bond with her child pales in comparison. The engraving on God's hands symbolizes a permanent, indelible connection. This is not passive memory; it's active, living, and sacred. Just as God's remembrance of his people is unwavering, so too our memories bind us to those we've lost, affirming their eternal significance.

These words display comfort: your child is remembered. You are remembered. Your love is recorded not just in journals and photos but in the heart of God. Memory is a holy place. You are right to visit it, to honor it, to live there when you need to. It is sacred ground. Within its confines, we find both the ache of absence and the warmth of presence. We find the duality of grief and gratitude, the bittersweet symphony of loss and love.

Consider the practices that sustain this sacred space—lighting candles, planting trees, creating art, sharing stories—each act is a thread woven into the tapestry of remembrance. These observances are not mere gestures; they are expressions of enduring love. They help shape a narrative where the presence of the departed is felt, honored, and celebrated.

Communities, too, play a role in this sacred remembering. When friends and family join in commemorating milestones, sharing memories, or simply sitting in silent support, they become part of the sacred ground. Their presence validates the grief and honors the memory, reinforcing that the life lost continues to ripple through the lives of others.

In Ps 77:11–12, the psalmist declares, "I will remember the deeds of the LORD; yes, I will remember your miracles of long ago. I will consider all your works and meditate on all your mighty deeds." Here, remembrance is both an act of worship and a source of strength. It's a deliberate choice to anchor oneself in the faithfulness and presence of God, especially during seasons of despair. This intentional remembering is mirrored in our personal grief journeys, where recalling the moments, voices, and lives of our loved ones sustains us.

Grief is not an enemy but an idea to have a conversation with it. It ebbs and flows, sometimes overwhelming, other times a gentle ache. Memory anchors us through these tides. It offers both refuge and reckoning, a place where we confront the depth of our loss and the breadth of our love. It teaches us that moving forward is not about forgetting but about integrating the loss into the story of our lives.

The sacredness of memory is reflected in cultures and traditions worldwide. From Día de los Muertos altars adorned with marigolds and photographs to Yahrzeit candles lit in Jewish homes, humanity has always sought ways to honor and remember.

These traditions affirm that remembering is not dwelling in the past but honoring the continuum of love.

In personal spaces, memory takes the form of keepsakes— a favorite book, a piece of clothing, a handwritten note. These objects are more than material; they are vessels of connection, carrying the essence of the one we miss. They remind us that the bond transcends physical presence. Nature, too, becomes a canvas for memory. A tree planted in remembrance grows, its branches reaching skyward, a living tribute. A star named in honor twinkles in the vast expanse, a cosmic reminder.

In sharing our memories, we invite others into the sacred space. We create a collective altar where stories intertwine and love multiplies. This shared remembrance fosters empathy, understanding, and a sense of connection. It breaks the isolation often felt in grief, replacing it with community and compassion.

As time passes, memory evolves. The sharp edges of early grief may soften, but the essence remains. New memories are built alongside the old, not replacing but complementing. The sacred ground expands, encompassing both the sorrow of loss and the joy of having loved.

To remember is to resist the erasure of what was meaningful. It is to stand firm in the truth that love endures. Memory is not just a personal sanctuary; it is a beacon shining light on lives that mattered, stories worth telling, and connections that transcend time.

In the end, memory is not a burden to carry but a gift to cherish. It is the sacred ground where we meet our loved ones, not as echoes of the past but as eternal companions of the heart. And in this holy place, we find that love never honestly says goodbye.

Key Reflection

- Grief and faith can coexist without contradiction.
- Jesus' lament invites us to bring our own sorrow into sacred space.
- Crying out is not the absence of faith—it is its fiercest expression.

Chapter 6—Memory Is a Holy Place

Close your eyes and return to a memory that brings warmth It may hurt, but let it be soft too.

- Whether you see memory as sacred, spiritual, or simply human, how do you honor the presence of the one you miss?
- What are some of your favorite memories of your child? Write them down in vivid detail.
- Are there certain days, songs, smells, or places that trigger powerful memories?
- How do you want others to remember your child's life?
- How might you create a small ritual or tradition to honor their memory each year?

CHAPTER 7

When Grief Lives in the Body

"The spirit of a man will sustain him in sickness,
but a broken spirit who can bear?"

—PROVERBS 18:14

G rief is not just emotional; it is biological and even cellular. When a child dies, the body keeps the score. The weight of loss settles deep into the bones, skin, and breath, embedding itself within the nervous system. Invisible scars etch themselves into muscles that tighten without warning, and fatigue lingers despite endless rest. Grief becomes a relentless companion, manifesting in ways both visible and hidden, tangible yet elusive.

It shows up in sleepless nights, even when exhaustion grips you, with a mind racing through memories and unanswerable questions. It presents as chest pains mimicking heart attacks, a crushing pressure embodying heartbreak's physical form. Brain fog turns the simplest tasks into daunting mountains, creating a sense of disconnection from the world around you. Random aches and unexplained illnesses surface as if grief has seeped into every cell, every fiber of your being. This is not weakness; it is the body's way of carrying a trauma too immense for words.

The psalmist understood this long before modern medicine, writing, "My tears have been my food day and night" (Ps 42:3). This lament reflects not only emotional sorrow but also the physical toll grief exacts. The psalmist is overwhelmed, consumed by grief to the point where sustenance is replaced by tears. This verse belongs to a larger context in Ps 42, where the author expresses a deep longing for God's presence amid despair. The psalm begins with, "As a deer longs for flowing streams, so my soul longs for you, O God" (verse 1). This imagery of thirst underscores an intense spiritual and emotional drought, highlighting how grief can create a chasm between us and the sense of divine closeness we once knew.

Delving into the broader context of Ps 42, we find a soul wrestling with feelings of abandonment and yearning for divine connection. The psalmist's repeated refrain, "Why, my soul, are you downcast? Why so disturbed within me? Put your hope in God, for I will yet praise him, my Savior and my God" (Ps 42:5, 11), reflects the cyclical nature of grief—oscillating between despair and hope. This internal dialogue is not a sign of spiritual weakness but an authentic expression of faith grappling with pain. The psalmist teaches us that faith is not the absence of sorrow but the courage to voice it honestly before God.

Also consider Ps 6, often referred to as a penitential psalm, where David cries out, "I am worn out from my groaning. All night long I flood my bed with weeping and drench my couch with tears" (Ps 6:6). This vivid imagery captures the exhaustive nature of grief—not merely emotional exhaustion but a holistic depletion affecting body, mind, and spirit. David's transparency before God models how we, too, can bring our tempestuous, unfiltered grief to God without fear of rejection.

Grief consumes energy, alters biochemistry, and reshapes neural pathways that once held joy and safety. Scientific research supports this, showing bereaved parents face higher risks of heart disease, immune dysfunction, depression, and even Takotsubo cardiomyopathy—known as broken heart syndrome.[1] This is not metaphorical but physiological; the heart can break under sorrow's weight. The psalmist's words are thus both poetic and scientifically prescient as they articulated the somatic experience of grief long before modern research confirmed it. Grief reshapes both body and soul, redefining your relationship with time, space, and identity.

Recognizing this is sacred knowledge. You are not merely "tired"; you are carrying the weight of eternity within a fragile human frame. Each breath is a testament to survival, a fragile thread connecting you to the world when everything inside feels unraveled. And yet, even in this grief, God is present—not demanding, not rushing, not rebuking, but simply present.

Consider the story of Elijah in 1 Kgs 19:4–8. After a triumphant victory over the prophets of Baal, Elijah flees into the wilderness, overwhelmed by fear and exhaustion, and prays for death under a broom tree. He says, "I have had enough, LORD. Take my life; I am no better than my ancestors" (1 Kgs 19:4). Elijah's despair is palpable, mirroring the depth of hopelessness that grief can bring. But God's response is not reprimand or dismissal. Instead, God sends an angel who gently wakes Elijah, providing food and water, saying, "Get up and eat, or the journey will be too much for you" (1 Kgs 19:7).

This divine encounter reveals God's tenderness in grief. There are no lectures, just sustenance and presence. Let your body be honored. Grief lives in your muscles, your breath, your bones. Take naps without guilt. Walk barefoot in the grass. These are traditions of self-compassion—your body remembers, so let it also be restored. Sometimes, survival means listening to your body, honoring your need for rest, weeping, and gentleness. It means granting yourself permission to exist in a state of brokenness without expectation or judgment. Progress is not linear, and grief defies timelines or stages, ebbing and flowing in waves—sometimes overwhelming, sometimes quiet, but always present. It requires rejecting societal demands to "bounce back" and

---

1. O'Connor, *Grieving Body*, 29–30.

choosing instead to move slowly, sacredly, in rhythm with your own battered heart. The pace of grief is deeply personal, necessitating patience and compassion.

Further reflecting on Scripture, consider Job's lament. In Job 3:11 he cries, "Why did I not die at birth, come forth from the womb and expire?" Job's unhindered anguish demonstrates that even the most righteous individuals are not immune to deep sorrow. His friends initially respond with silent companionship—a powerful testament to the ministry of presence. It's only when they begin to offer explanations that their comfort falters. This narrative teaches us the importance of sitting with grief without the compulsion to "fix" it.

The body carries grief, but it also holds memory and love. It bears the sacred rage that propels you forward when every cell screams to give up. This rage is not destructive; it is sacred—a fierce, unyielding force that defies despair, insists on remembering, honoring, and surviving. Your body is not your enemy; it is the last temple where your child's memory resides. Every heartbeat, breath, and tear is a testament to that love, deserving of mercy not because grief demands it but because love does.

Consider small acts of care as sacred inclination: drinking water as an offering to sustain the temple, resting when weary as an act of reverence, and allowing tears to fall freely as a baptism cleansing the soul's wounds. The book of Job offers reflections on grief and sacred rage. In Job 3:26, Job laments, "I have no peace, no quietness; I have no rest, but only turmoil." Here, the honesty of Job's anguish is not dismissed but held within the sacred narrative, illustrating that divine engagement is not absent in our turmoil but deeply embedded within it. This acknowledgment affirms that God presence does not require our completeness but resonates powerfully within our fragmented experiences, guiding us toward a sacred reorientation of the soul.

Grief doesn't diminish with time; it integrates, weaving itself into your being—not as an intruder but as a testament to the depth of your love. You learn to carry it, not because it becomes lighter but because you grow stronger—not through the absence of pain but in the enduring presence of love.

Even in the darkest nights, when despair feels absolute, there is something sacred in simply existing. Your breath, though ragged, is a prayer; your heartbeat, though heavy, is a song of survival. In quiet moments, when grief feels too vast to hold, remember you are not alone. Your pain is seen, and your love is eternal. Grief is not a problem to solve but a story to honor—an echo of love so strong, deep, and profound it left an imprint on your very being.

Be gentle with yourself. Rest when needed, cry when you must, and rage when silence feels unbearable. Know beyond doubt: your body, weary and broken as it may feel, is a holy vessel. It carries not just grief but the enduring, unbreakable bond of love.

Key Reflection

- Grief and faith can coexist without contradiction.

- Jesus' lament invites us to bring our own sorrow into sacred space.

- Crying out is not the absence of faith—it is its fiercest expression.

Chapter 7—When Grief Lives in the Body

- How has your body changed since your loss? What symptoms have you noticed?

- How do you treat yourself on days when your grief feels physical?

- What are gentle, loving practices you can offer your body (rest, nature, breathing, prayer)?

- How does it feel to think of your body as carrying both grief and sacred memory?

CHAPTER 8

Sacred Rage, Sacred Love: Living Forward with Both

The soul would have no rainbow
if the eyes had no tears.

—NATIVE AMERICAN PROVERB

W e've already explored sacred rage as the protest of love. Now we turn to how this rage evolves—how it holds hands with sacred love and teaches us to live forward. In grief's fire, what remains is not just ash but ember: a spark of love that refuses to die. Let us now examine how rage does not cancel faith but deepens it.

The Theological Foundation of Sacred Rage and Sacred Love

The Bible is replete with narratives that embody the duality of sacred rage and sacred love. In exploring the Psalms, we find expressions of human emotion that vacillate between lament and praise. Psalm 13 is a testament to this, beginning with the anguished cry, "How long, O LORD? Will you forget me forever?" (verse 1) yet concluding with, "But I trust in your unfailing love; my heart rejoices in your salvation" (verse 5). Here, the psalmist does not resolve his pain through dismissal but through an honest dialogue with God, embracing both despair and trust.

Job: The Archetype of Grief and Divine Dialogue

Job's narrative offers an expansive view of sacred rage. His loss was catastrophic, yet his response was not subdued piety but candid confrontation. In Job 7:17–18, he challenges God: "What is mankind that you make so much of them, that you give them so much attention, that you examine them every morning and test them every moment?" Job's audacity in grief is not condemned but included in sacred Scripture, validating the place of questioning and anger in faithful living. God's eventual response, found in Job 38, does not chastise Job for his boldness but expands his perspective, indicating that divine relationship encompasses our deepest sorrows and fiercest questions. This narrative illustrates that authentic faith can coexist with—and even be deepened by—honest struggle and sentiment.

Jesus: The Embodiment of Sacred Emotions

The New Testament continues this theme vividly in the life of Jesus. His response to injustice and loss was anything but passive. In Matt 21:12–13, Jesus drives out the money changers from the temple with righteous indignation, declaring, "My house will be called a house of prayer, but you are making it 'a den of robbers.'" This sacred rage was not devoid of love; it was love's fierce defense of what was sacred.

At the heart of grief, the words from Isa 53:3 resonate deeply: "[God] was despised and rejected, a being of suffering, and familiar with pain." This Scripture unveils a divine presence that does not remain distant from sorrow but is intimately acquainted with our deepest wounds. The phrase "a being of suffering" conveys more than passive empathy—it reflects an active participation in human anguish, embodying both the weight of heartache and the sacred rage against the injustices intertwined with death.

Sacred rage, in this context, is not a rejection of faith but a manifestation of it. It recognizes the harsh reality that death, particularly the loss of children, often feels like a profound injustice. This rage is not directed at God but at the brokenness of the world—a cry for restoration and justice. It is the soul's protest against the unnatural rupture that death brings, affirming that such grief is not a sign of spiritual weakness but a testament to the depth of love and the yearning for wholeness.

The death of children confronts us with the starkest sense of injustice, challenging our theological frameworks. Yet, in these moments, God does not offer platitudes but presence. God stands with us, embodying both the grief and the sacred indignation that such losses evoke. This duality reassures us that our sorrow is acknowledged, our rage is valid, and our hope is rooted in a divine empathy that has walked the path of suffering alongside humanity.

Ecclesiastes and the Seasonality of Grief

Ecclesiastes 3:1–8 radically acknowledges life's emotional and experiential rhythms. The declaration that "there is a time for everything" invites us to honor each season, including the contradictory coexistence of mourning and dancing, weeping and laughing. Grief is not a linear process but cyclical, where sacred rage and sacred love ebb and flow, much like the changing seasons.

The Prophets: Voices of Sacred Protest

The prophets of the Old Testament often voiced sacred rage against societal injustices, echoing God's own dissatisfaction with oppression and wrongdoing. Amos 5:24 boldly proclaims, "But let justice roll on like a river, righteousness like a never-failing stream!" This prophetic outcry is born from a deep love for God's people and a sacred intolerance for their suffering. The prophetic tradition teaches us that sacred rage can be a divine instrument for justice, not merely a human reaction.

Sacred Practices: Rituals of Rage and Love

Incorporating rituals can help navigate the landscape of these intense emotions. The act of lament, as practiced in biblical times, involved communal expressions of grief, sackcloth, and ashes—outward signs that sorrow was not to be hidden but shared. Today, lighting candles, creating art, writing letters to the departed, or even physical expressions like shouting into the wilderness or pounding the earth, can serve as modern-day rituals that honor both sacred rage and sacred love.

Modern Reflections Through Scriptural Lens

Psalm 88, often regarded as one of the darkest psalms because it ends without words of hope, is included in Scripture for a reason. It validates the experience of enduring darkness without immediate resolution. This inclusion teaches us that the Bible does not shy away from the full spectrum of human emotion but embraces it as part of the sacred narrative.

The Cross: Ultimate Intersection of Rage and Love

At the heart of Christian faith is the cross—a symbol where sacred rage against sin and death meets the sacred love of God's redemptive act. Jesus' cry, "My God, my God, why have you forsaken me?" (Matt 27:46), echoes the psalms of lament and stands as a testament to the authenticity of expressing anguish, even unto God. Yet, this moment of despair is enveloped within the larger narrative of resurrection, where love triumphs.

Conclusion: Living with the Paradox

To live in the aftermath of an enormous loss is to dwell in the paradox where sacred rage and sacred love are not sequential stages but concurrent truths. The Scriptures don't compel us to choose one over the other but rather invite us to hold both with reverence. As Rom 8:26–27 reminds us, "Likewise the Spirit helps us in our weakness; for we do not know how to pray as we ought, but that very Spirit intercedes with sighs too deep for words. And God, who searches hearts, knows what is the mind of the Spirit, because the Spirit intercedes for the saints according to the will of God." This passage illustrates the interplay between grief and sacred fervor, providing a theological perspective through which we comprehend our inner struggles. It speaks to the Spirit's intimate companionship in our brokenness, guiding us toward awareness and transformation beyond mere endurance.

Grief often feels like standing at the intersection of sacred rage and sacred love—both fierce and tender, both cries of protest and whispers of hope. Sacred rage is not defiance against God but an acknowledgment of the world's brokenness, a reflection of God's own grief over injustice. It is a sacred echo of the cry against what should not be, including the heart-wrenching loss that seems unjust, like the death of a child.

Yet, even in the throes of such loss, sacred love persists. It does not erase grief or negate sacred rage; instead, it exists alongside them, affirming that we are not abandoned in our sorrow. The Divine's presence is unwavering, holding us through the storm, not as a distant observer but as an intimate companion feeling the depths of our pain.

Thus, grief, sacred rage, and sacred love form a holy trinity of response to loss, each holding space for the other. They remind us that our lament is not a lack of faith but an expression of it, a testament to the depth of our love and the sense of injustice when life is cut short, especially so tender and full of potential.

In embracing this duality, we find a reflection of the divine heart—vast enough to contain the full breadth of human experience.

Sacred rage. Sacred love. Sacred life, rising continuously from the ashes, bearing witness to a love that endures beyond the grave.

Key Reflection

- Grief and faith can coexist without contradiction.
- Jesus' lament invites us to bring our own sorrow into sacred space.
- Crying out is not the absence of faith—it is its fiercest expression.

Chapter 8—Sacred Rage, Sacred Love: Living Forward with Both

- When you feel rage, what specific memories, injustices, or moments come to mind?
- When you feel love, what memories or emotions rise to the surface?
- How might you honor both your anger and your love without feeling like you have to "fix" or silence either one?
- Write a letter to your child that holds both the rage and the love together.

CHAPTER 9

The Sacred Work of Living Forward

Though I fall, I will rise again; though I sit in darkness,
the LORD will be my light.

—MICAH 7:8

There is no returning to "normal." There is only forward. But forward does not mean forgetting; it means choosing to live in a world that broke you while carrying the love that built you. It's about taking each fragile step with the echoes of loss reverberating in your soul yet allowing the light of cherished memories to guide your path. Forward is not a destination but a journey—a continuous process of navigating the rough waters of grief while holding tightly to the anchors of love and hope.

To live forward after the death of a child is to live in defiance of despair. It is a bold, courageous act—a quiet revolution against the crushing weight of sorrow. It's not about closing the chapter, as if grief were a story with a tidy ending. Instead, it's about learning how to write with a broken pen, on a torn page, and with a heart that beats despite its fractures. The ink may smudge with tears, the words may tremble with pain, but the narrative continues because your love for your child never ends. This love becomes the ink with which you write the next chapters—messy, uninhibited, and authentic chapters that reflect both the depth of your loss and the enduring strength of your spirit.

Living forward means embracing the full spectrum of your emotions without judgment. It means getting through days when the ache is unbearable, when breathing feels like an effort, and when the silence screams louder than any noise. It's about building new memories without guilt, allowing yourself to smile and feel warmth without the shadow of "I shouldn't be happy" looming over you. Finding beauty in unexpected places and letting it coexist with your pain is also part of this journey. The laughter you share, the sunsets you admire, and the small joys you stumble upon do not diminish your grief; instead, they illuminate the resilience of the human heart. Speaking their name in the present tense honors their impact, acknowledging that their life and love continue to shape you, even in their physical absence.

This is sacred work—not the kind the world applauds with standing ovations or accolades, but the kind heaven records with reverence. It's the sacred act of choosing life, even when every fiber of your being aches with absence. It honors the love that was, the love that is, and the love that remains eternal. To live forward is not to move on from grief—it is to let grief shape you without erasing you. Grief carves deep valleys in your heart, but within those valleys, seeds of resilience, compassion, and understanding can grow. These seeds, though born from sorrow, have the potential to blossom into agents of empathy for others, a deeper appreciation for life's fleeting moments, and an unshakable strength rooted in survival.

The Bible never says you must "get over it." There's no verse demanding you tie your grief into a neat bow and tuck it away. Instead, it invites us into transformation, acknowledging human suffering and offering comfort in God's presence amid our pain. As Paul writes, "We are hard pressed on every side, but not crushed; perplexed, but not in despair; persecuted, but not abandoned; struck down, but not destroyed" (2 Cor 4:8–9). These words resonate deeply for those navigating loss, affirming that while grief can press us down, it cannot completely crush the essence of who we are. Our spirits, though battered, endure because they are held by a love greater than our pain.

Consider the words from the book of Job, where Job's lament and struggle capture the essence of human grief and sacred outrage. In Job 19:25–27, Job proclaims, "I know that my redeemer lives, and that in the end he will stand on the earth. And after my skin has been destroyed, yet in my flesh I will see God." This passage does not shy away from the depths of suffering; instead, it confronts it head-on, affirming the enduring presence of God amid desolation. Job's declarations mirror the intensity of loss and the fervor of questioning, illustrating how grief and sacred defiance can reside side by side. His words offer a testament that even in the middle of despair, there exists an unwavering connection to God—one that persists beyond our temporal afflictions, anchoring us in the sacred continuity of hope beyond comprehension.

In Isa 53:3, the prophecy about Jesus describes him as "a man of sorrows, acquainted with grief." This powerful depiction reminds us that even Christ experienced intense grief during his time on earth. His tears at the tomb of his friend Lazarus (John 11:35) show that grief is not a sign of weakness or a lack of faith—it is a natural, human response to loss. Jesus wept, even though he knew he would raise Lazarus from the dead, illustrating that acknowledging grief is not incompatible with hope. His empathy for Mary and Martha's sorrow reveals a God who does not shy away from our pain but steps into it with us, offering comfort through his presence.

The book of Lamentations offers another testament to the coexistence of grief and hope. Written in the aftermath of Jerusalem's devastation, it is a collection of laments. Yet, amid the sorrow, Jeremiah writes, "Because of the LORD's great love we are not consumed, for his compassions never fail. They are new every morning; great is your faithfulness" (Lam 3:22–23). This passage reminds us that even in the depths of despair, God's faithfulness remains a source of renewal. Each sunrise carries the promise of new mercies, a quiet testament to the enduring presence of divine compassion, even when the shadows of grief feel overwhelming.

Paul also acknowledges the complexity of grief in 1 Thess 4:13: "But we do not want you to be uninformed, brothers and sisters, about those who have died, so that you may not grieve as others do who have no hope." Notice that Paul does not say simply, "Do not grieve"—he recognizes grief as inevitable. Instead, he encourages grieving with hope, anchored in the resurrection promise. This hope does not erase the pain but offers a sacred perspective: death is not the final word. The bonds of love stretch beyond the veil, held together by the promise of eternal reunion.

Moreover, in Rom 8:38–39, Paul reassures us of God's unwavering love: "For I am convinced that neither death nor life, neither angels nor demons, neither the present nor the future, nor any powers . . . will be able to separate us from the love of God that is in Christ Jesus our Lord." This powerful declaration affirms that even in death, love endures. The connection we have with our loved ones is not severed by physical absence because God's love transcends all boundaries. This eternal love serves as a bridge, linking hearts across time and space, whispering that while our loved ones are gone from sight, they are never gone from our hearts.

In Rev 21:4, we are given a vision of ultimate restoration: "He will wipe every tear from their eyes. Death will be no more; mourning and crying and pain will be no more, for the first things have passed away." While this promise speaks of a future hope, it also provides comfort in the present, reminding us that our grief is temporary in the grand narrative of eternity. The day will come when loss is no more, when every tear shed in sorrow will be tenderly wiped away by the very hand of God.

Living forward with grief requires courage, faith, and the willingness to hold both sorrow and hope in the same heart. It is a sacred journey—a testament to the enduring power of love. The Scriptures do not offer quick fixes or simple answers, but they do offer companionship, understanding, and the assurance of God's presence in every season of our lives. They remind us that grief is not a detour from faith but part of the sacred landscape where God meets us with gentle grace.

When we walk through the valley of the shadow of death, as Ps 23:4 describes, we do so with the promise that we are not alone: "I will fear no evil, for you are with me; your rod and your staff, they comfort me." This verse doesn't promise the absence of dark valleys but assures us of God's presence within them. His rod and staff symbolize both guidance and protection, gentle reminders that even when our path winds through sorrow, we are never abandoned.

Therefore, to live forward is to walk hand in hand with grief, guided by faith, buoyed by love, and sustained by hope. It is to write new chapters while honoring the ones that came before, knowing that every word penned, every tear shed, and every breath taken is part of a sacred narrative that God holds with gentle reverence. In this narrative, your grief is not a flaw to be fixed but a testament to a love that was deep, true, and transformative—a love that continues to echo in the chambers of your heart, shaping the story of your life with sacred significance.

Key Reflection

- Grief and faith can coexist without contradiction.
- Jesus' lament invites us to bring our own sorrow into sacred space.
- Crying out is not the absence of faith—it is its fiercest expression.

Chapter 9—The Sacred Work of Living Forward

Breathe deeply. You have made it this far.
Let that be enough for now.

- In what ways can living forward honor—not replace—the love that still pulses in your soul? What does moving forward mean to you, in your own time and way?

- What does "living forward" look like for you right now? What does it *not* look like?

- In what ways have you changed—emotionally, spiritually, relationally—since your loss?

- What do you want the world to know about your child and how they still impact your life?

- How does your vision of the future look different since your loss—and what does hope now mean to you?

- How will you honor your child's memory in the way you live, love, and serve?

CHAPTER 10

When the World Moves On Without You

Joy is not in things; it is in us.

—RICHARD WAGNER

P salm 30:11–12 states, "You turned my mourning into dancing; you removed my sackcloth and clothed me with joy, that my heart may sing your praises and not be silent. LORD my God, I will praise you forever." This powerful Scripture is imbued with holy meaning, providing spiritual strength, consolation, and the hope of God's abiding presence to those journeying through the depths of grief. To fully grasp the depth of this passage, it's essential to explore its historical, cultural, and spiritual context, as well as its relevance to our personal journeys through sorrow and stability.

Psalm 30 is attributed to King David, a man whose life was a tapestry woven with threads of triumph, failure, joy, and despair. David experienced the full spectrum of human emotions—he was a shepherd, a warrior, a fugitive, a king, and a man after God's own heart. His psalms reflect his intimate relationship with God, marked by honesty and deep faith. It is believed that Ps 30 was composed as a song of dedication, to commemorate the dedication of the temple, though David himself did not build it. His son Solomon would eventually fulfill that task. Nonetheless, David's heart was deeply connected to the concept of the temple as a dwelling place for God's presence.

The phrase "you turned my mourning into dancing" is not just poetic imagery; it speaks to a radical transformation. In biblical times, mourning was a visibly communal act. People expressed grief openly and publicly. They wore sackcloth—a coarse, uncomfortable material made from goat's hair—as a symbol of their inner anguish. Sackcloth was often accompanied by ashes, which mourners would sprinkle on their heads or sit among, signifying deep sorrow and repentance. Mourning rituals included wailing, weeping, fasting, and even hiring professional mourners to vocalize the depth of loss. This was not a private, hidden emotion but a shared, acknowledged experience within the community.

When David proclaims that God turned his mourning into dancing, he is testifying to an extraordinary shift—not merely an easing of sorrow but a complete reversal. God didn't just comfort David; he transformed his reality. The heavy, scratchy sackcloth symbolizing grief was replaced with garments of joy. This change signifies more than a superficial improvement. It reflects a reassurance of inner renewal. It's the difference between surviving and truly living again.

This theme is echoed throughout Scripture, reinforcing the idea that while grief is a natural and necessary part of life, it is not the concluding chapter. Consider Isa 61:3, which promises "to provide for those who mourn in Zion—to give them a garland instead of ashes, the oil of gladness instead of mourning, the mantle of praise instead of a faint spirit." This divine exchange—ashes for beauty and mourning for joy—is not about dismissing grief but about the transformative power of God's grace. It acknowledges the pain while offering hope for renewal.

In the New Testament, Jesus embodies this promise. In the Beatitudes, he declares, "Blessed are those who mourn, for they will be comforted" (Matt 5:4). This is not a vague, conditional comfort; it is a guaranteed assurance. Jesus' words highlight that mourning is not a sign of weakness or a lack of faith. Instead, it is an honest response to loss, and it is in this vulnerable space that God's comfort meets us most. The comfort he offers does not erase the pain but infuses it with his presence, bringing peace that surpasses human understanding (Phil 4:7).

As we navigate our own journeys through grief, these Scriptures become anchors for our souls. They remind us that "though you sow in tears, you will reap with songs of joy" (Ps 126:5). This joy is not dependent on external circumstances; it is rooted in the unchanging character of God. God is "a refuge and strength, an ever-present help in trouble" (Ps 46:1).

It's important to recognize that the journey from mourning to dancing is not linear. There will be days when the ache feels overwhelming, when the weight of loss presses heavily on our hearts. There may be moments when laughter feels foreign, even inappropriate. Yet, even in these dark valleys, God is at work. He gently stitches our broken hearts, mends the torn fabric of our lives, and prepares us to carry both grief and joy simultaneously.

Second Corinthians 4:8–9 offers an additional reflection: "We are hard pressed on every side, but not crushed; perplexed, but not in despair; persecuted, but not abandoned; struck down, but not destroyed." This passage speaks to the enduring spirit within us, even amid grief and sacred rage. It acknowledges the weight of suffering while affirming that it does not define or consume us fully.

In the unrestrained forms of grief, our souls search for meaning in God's unwavering presence. Second Corinthians 4:8–9 speaks to the heart's cry in times of loss, illustrating that while pain may press upon us, it does not sever our connection to the sacred. The Divine's assurance permeates our struggles, offering an anchoring force.

In this sacred struggle, we encounter a depth—a space not of simple comfort but of transformative anchorage. Grief reshapes us, yet the divine narrative within us remains unbroken, an enduring testament to the strength carried through our faith. This passage does not merely soothe; it illuminates the unyielding thread of divine companionship woven through our trials.

Sometimes, guilt creeps in when we find ourselves laughing after a loss. It whispers that our joy is a betrayal, that moving forward means forgetting. But these Scriptures speak louder. Laughter is not a denial of grief; it is a testament to love's enduring power. Joy does not mean we've forgotten; it means we're learning to live with the loss in a new way. We carry our loved ones in our hearts, their memories woven into the essence of our daily lives.

Isaiah 57:1-2 offers a reflection on the mysteries of life and death: "The righteous perish, and no one takes it to heart; the devout are taken away, and no one understands that the righteous are taken away to be spared from evil. Those who walk uprightly enter into peace; they find rest as they lie in death." This passage speaks to the perplexing nature of loss, particularly when it feels unjust, such as the death of children. It reminds us that what appears as an injustice from our earthly perspective may, in the divine tapestry, hold layers of mercy and grace beyond our comprehension.

Grief and sacred rage often walk hand in hand, particularly when faced with loss. Sacred rage is not a defiance against God but rather an honest outpouring of the heart—a reflection of our deep connection to the sacredness of life. It is an acknowledgment of the brokenness in the world and a yearning for the justice and wholeness that our souls instinctively know should exist.

In these moments, theological reassurance comes from understanding that grief is not a sign of weak faith, nor is righteous anger a departure from spiritual trust. Both are deeply rooted in our humanity and our divine image-bearing. The coexistence of grief and sacred rage forms a sacred space where we wrestle with the complexities of loss, seeking comfort not in easy answers but in the presence of God, who embraces all our emotions without judgment.

The apostle Paul reflects this paradox in 2 Cor 6:10, describing himself as "sorrowful, yet always rejoicing." This tension is the heart of the human experience. We can hold sorrow in one hand and joy in the other, honoring both. This duality does not diminish our love for those we've lost; it honors it by acknowledgeing the depth of our emotions.

The resurrection of Jesus is the ultimate demonstration of this truth. On Good Friday, his followers faced crushing grief, their hopes buried with him. But that grief was not the end of the story. On Easter morning, joy burst forth—not because the pain of Friday was forgotten but because love had triumphed over death. This is the hope we cling to in our own seasons of loss.

Philippians 4:4 encourages us to "rejoice in the Lord always. I will say it again: Rejoice!" Paul wrote these words from prison, facing uncertainty and hardship. His joy was not rooted in circumstances but in the unshakable foundation of God's presence and promises. This kind of joy is resilient. It does not ignore pain but rises above it, grounded in a reality greater than our current suffering.

In John 16:22, Jesus comforts his disciples with these words: "So with you: Now is your time of grief, but I will see you again and you will rejoice, and no one will take away your joy." This promise of joy is eternal, secured by the hope of reunion. For those who grieve, this assurance brings comfort. Our separation from loved ones is temporary; the love remains eternal.

Psalm 126:5–6 adds another layer to this theme: "Those who sow with tears will reap with songs of joy. Those who go out weeping, carrying seed to sow, will return with songs of joy, carrying sheaves with them." Our tears are not wasted. They water the seeds of remembrance and hope, which will one day bear the fruit of joy. This imagery reminds us that even in our sorrow, there is purpose, and in time, joy will blossom again.

Reflecting on these Scriptures, we see a consistent message: grief and joy are not opposites but companions on the journey of life. Mourning is sacred, and so is the joy that follows. Both are expressions of a heart that has loved deeply. When laughter returns, let it rise without guilt. Let it be a tribute—a melody woven with threads of memory, love, and hope. When joy finds you, welcome it as an old friend who has walked with you through the valley and knows the depths of your heart.

Your loved one's memory is deeply ingrained in your very being, and nothing, not even time, distance, or death, can erase it. Their legacy lives on in your courage, resilience, and willingness to find beauty in brokenness. This legacy serves as a beacon, a testament to their enduring impact on your life.

This is sacred ground—the intersection of grief and joy, where love's story continues to unfold. Your laughter is not a betrayal; it's a celebration. Your joy is not forgetting; it's remembering in the most beautiful way possible. This remembrance is a living testament to love's endurance.

So, live forward—not with guilt but with grace. Carry their light with you—not as a burden but as a beacon. Dance, laugh, dream again—not because the pain is gone but because love still lives. In living fully, you honor them more deeply than you could ever imagine. This is the sacred journey of courageousness and remembrance.

Key Reflection

- Grief and faith can coexist without contradiction.
- Jesus' lament invites us to bring our own sorrow into sacred space.
- Crying out is not the absence of faith—it is its fiercest expression.

Chapter 10—When the World Moves On Without You

- When was the first time you felt even a moment of happiness after your loss?
- What emotions rose up—joy, guilt, fear, hope?
- How does it feel to think of joy as a way to honor your child's memory, not erase it?
- What small acts of joy could you fight for today, without guilt?

CHAPTER 11

Fighting for Joy Without Guilt

"Let each of us contribute to the good of the whole; let the strong care for the weak, and the weak respect the strong; let the wealthy provide for the poor, and the poor give thanks to God."

—1 CLEMENT 38:2

One of the cruelest shocks of grief is how quickly the world forgets. In the immediate aftermath of loss, there is an outpouring of support. At first, there are flowers—vivid bouquets meant to offer comfort, their fleeting beauty a fragile attempt to counterbalance the permanence of loss. Cards with handwritten notes bearing heartfelt condolences arrive, each word trying to bridge the chasm of absence. Texts flood in, filled with words like "thinking of you" and "I'm here if you need anything," simple phrases holding both genuine care and the helplessness of not knowing what to say.

Prayers are whispered, offered in quiet corners, candles lit in honor of the one who is no longer here. And then—silence. The world resumes its rhythm. People who once stood vigil at your door—bearing casseroles, warm hugs, and tearful solidarity—return to their daily routines. Conversations shift back to the trivial, to weather forecasts, office gossip, upcoming vacations.

The chatter of life continues unabated, and laughter—bright and uninhibited—feels too loud, too fast, too careless. It pierces the stillness you've been wrapped in, a reminder that life elsewhere remains untouched by the storm that has ravaged yours. And you are left holding the shattered pieces of your life, wondering how everyone else is breathing so easily. Each breath feels like an act of rebellion against the reality of your loss, and yet, you continue because there's no other choice.

Sacred Rage and the Scriptural Response

Sacred rage rises here too. It bubbles under the surface, not as bitterness but as a fierce testament to love's enduring nature. It's not the rage of resentment; it's the rage of a parent who knows that love does not have an expiration date. You rage because the world dares to move on while you are still bleeding. The wound is fresh, unveiled, and unhealed, and society's expectation for you to "find closure" feels like a demand to erase the significance of what was lost.

You rage because society demands "strength" when what you need is permission to simply exist—fragile, broken, and unapologetically grieving. This sacred rage speaks truths that often go unheard: "Do not rush me to heal. Healing is not linear, and grief is not a task to be completed." "Do not erase my child because remembering is uncomfortable for you. Their existence matters beyond the confines of your comfort zone."

> *"Do not pretend their life was a chapter when it was my whole book. Every page of my heart is written with their name."*

In Matt 14, when John the Baptist was executed, Jesus did not dismiss the sorrow or tell his disciples to "move on." He did not offer empty words or simple reassurances. Instead, Jesus withdrew to a solitary place to grieve, honoring the depth of loss (Matt 14:13).

This act speaks volumes—God incarnate did not avoid the pain, did not rush past the sorrow, did not minimize the grief.

Grief is sacred space, and even God entered into it with full presence. This sacred grief holds theological weight, intertwining with what some call "sacred rage"—a deep, righteous response to the brokenness of the world, to injustices such as the death of children, which often feels unbearably unjust. Sacred rage is not about vengeance but about a heart aligned with divine justice, aching for what should have been whole.

When a child is lost, it feels like a cosmic tear in the fiber of life itself, defying our sense of fairness. Yet, even in that unbearable ache, God is not distant. The Divine grieves with us, acknowledging the injustice without diminishing it. They hold space for both sorrow and the hope that such pain goes unseen by the One who embodies love and justice.

Consider the broader context of John 11. When Jesus arrives in Bethany, he finds that Lazarus has already been in the tomb for four days. Martha meets him first, saying, "Lord, if you had been here, my brother would not have died" (John 11:21). Her words are not just filled with sorrow but with an undercurrent of frustration and sacred rage. She believes in Jesus' power but wrestles with his absence in her moment of dire need.

Jesus responds not with rebuke but with truth and empathy. He declares, "I am the resurrection and the life" (John 11:25), anchoring her hope in the eternal, even amid her temporal grief. Yet, he does not dismiss her pain. Instead, he meets Mary, who echoes her sister's lament (John 11:32), and upon seeing her weeping, "He was deeply moved in spirit and troubled" (John 11:33). The Greek term used here (*embrimaomai*) conveys a unique emotional response, a mixture of indignation and compassion.[1]

Jesus' tears at Lazarus's tomb are not just for his friend but also for the pain sin and death have inflicted upon humanity. They are sacred tears that validate human grief. If Christ himself could

---

1. Danker et al., "ἐμβριμάομαι," in *Greek-English Lexicon*, 323–24. See also Keener, *Gospel of John*, 846–47, for a contextual interpretation linking Jesus' indignation to compassion in John 11.

stop and grieve, then you are not wrong for feeling sacred anger when others move on too soon. You are not petty for holding onto memories that refuse to fade.

God's Compassion in the Depths of Loss

You are not weak for breaking under the strain of absence. You are carrying a love the world cannot measure, a love that does not diminish with time or distance. And in the quiet spaces where others forget, God still remembers. When the phone stops ringing, when the cards stop coming, and when the world no longer marks the dates that are seared into your heart, God still draws near.

Consider Job 23:8–10: "But if I go to the east, he is not there; if I go to the west, I do not find him. When he is at work in the north, I do not see him; when he turns to the south, I catch no glimpse of him. But he knows the way that I take; when he has tested me, I will come forth as gold." This passage is more than a distant reflection—it's an intricate portrayal of divine proximity amid absence. Job's lament resonates deeply with the soul's struggle during grief and sacred rage, capturing the paradox of feeling forsaken while being intimately known.

Job's narrative unfolds in the crucible of loss and bewilderment, where his cries echo through the silence of heaven. His experiences articulate a theological truth: God is not diminished by our questions or anger. Instead, God's engagement with Job's anguish reveals an enduring companionship that transcends circumstance. Job's words teach us that transformation occurs not through the eradication of pain but within the furnace of sorrow itself, forging depth and clarity in the soul's journey.

Yet, David often concludes his laments with remembrance of God's faithfulness. This juxtaposition teaches us that faith and grief coexist. Sacred rage and sacred trust are not mutually exclusive. You do not have to race grief. There is no finish line, no prize for "moving on" faster. You do not have to silence your sorrow to make others comfortable. Your grief is not too much; it is the natural response to a love that runs deep.

Anchored by Sacred Memory

You do not have to pretend your child's absence has become "normal." There is no normal in the wake of such loss—only a new landscape you are forced to navigate. Sacred rage will keep you honest. It refuses to let you diminish your pain for the sake of others' ease. It stands as a testament to the depth of your love, a fierce declaration that your child mattered, matters still, and will always matter.

Sacred memory will keep you anchored. It holds the precious fragments of what was, cradles the echoes of laughter, the warmth of touch, the light in their eyes. And God will keep you even when the world does not. When the world moves on, he remains. When friends grow silent, he listens. When you feel invisible in your grief, he sees. His love does not fade with time, does not diminish with distance.

The Sacredness of Grief in God's Eyes

Grief is not a problem to be solved. It is a journey to be honored. It reshapes you, carves out new spaces within you, and teaches you how to carry both joy and sorrow in the same breath. Consider Isa 61:1–3: "The spirit of the Lord GOD is upon me because the LORD has anointed me . . . to bring good news to the oppressed, to bind up the brokenhearted, to proclaim liberty to the captives and release to the prisoners, . . . to comfort all who mourn, to provide for those who grieve in Zion—to give them a garland instead of ashes, the oil of gladness instead of mourning, and the mantle of praise instead of a faint spirit." Your grief has its season, and it is sacred.

Grief, especially in the face of the death of children, feels like the very thread of justice is torn. Sacred rage arises from this space—not to be confused with wrath but as a response to the deep rupture in the human heart when confronted with such loss. Sacred rage acknowledges the injustice of death's timing and the ache of absence, yet it also calls us to remember that grief and rage are not void of divine presence. They echo the divine grief over suffering and loss in the world. Theologically, sacred rage is an expression of love's depth, a testament to the value and irreplaceable worth of the one lost. In this, we find reassurance: our grief is not foreign to God. It is held, honored, and met with a promise of comfort, and remembered.

It is sacred, this aching love, and it deserves to be met with kindness, patience, and reverence. So let your sacred rage rise. Let it be a beacon, a burning testament to the love that remains. Let your sacred memory guide you, anchoring you in the truth of your child's and/or loved one's life, the indelible mark they left on your heart.

And when the world forgets, remember this: God still remembers. God weeps with you. God rages with you. God holds you when the weight is too much to bear. You are not alone. You are seen. You are loved. And your grief is sacred.

Key Reflection

- Grief and faith can coexist without contradiction.

- Jesus' lament invites us to bring our own sorrow into sacred space.

- Crying out is not the absence of faith—it is its fiercest expression.

Chapter 11—Fighting for Joy Without Guilt

- How have you experienced others "moving on" before you were ready?

- What emotions rise when you think about the world's expectation for you to be "better" by now?

- How do you honor your child's memory even when others stop mentioning their name?

- What would you say if you could write a letter to the world about grief's timeline?

Reflection and Journaling

Chapter 1—The Day the World Broke

- What memories stand out most from the day your world changed?

- How do you feel when you think about that day? Sadness? Rage? Numbness? Something else?

- If you could say anything to yourself on the day your world broke, what would it be?

- Where, even in the smallest ways, have you seen traces of God's presence after that day?

Chapter 2—Sacred Rage: The Love That Refused to Die

- Whether or not you believe in God today, what would it look like to trust love again—even if it's fierce, even if it's angry?

- What angers you most about your loss?

- Have you ever been made to feel ashamed of your anger? By yourself? By others?

- What would it feel like to believe that your rage is seen —and even held—by the sacred?

- If God feels far, what language or presence do you wish could hold your pain?

- What tables would you turn over if you could, in honor of your child's life?

Chapter 3—Their Name: A Name Written in Eternity

- If you do not believe in a divine afterlife, what does it mean to let their legacy live through you? What is love's role in remembrance?

- What are the moments when your child's memory feels closest to you?

- How has your love for them changed, deepened, or grown even after their passing?

- What sacred rituals, prayers, or traditions might you create to honor their ongoing presence in your life?

- How has your child's memory shaped your purpose or redefined what matters most in your life?

- Write a letter to your child, telling them how you carry their love forward.

Chapter 4—When Faith Feels like a Lie

- Have you ever felt abandoned by God during your grief?

- What words or phrases meant to "comfort" you actually made the pain feel worse?

- What honest prayer would you pray today if you believed God could handle your anger?

- How has your understanding of faith changed since your loss?

Chapter 5—Learning to Breathe Again: Tiny Acts of Survival

- What does surviving mean for you today? How does your breath carry the memory of love forward, even when your strength feels small?

- What are the small acts of survival you've managed that others might not even notice?

- What tiny victories have you experienced since your loss, even if they seemed insignificant at the time?

- What parts of your identity have changed through surviving this loss? How do you see yourself now?

- How do you talk to yourself on the hard days—are you kind, patient, harsh?

- What does it mean to you to think of survival itself as sacred?

Chapter 6—Memory Is a Holy Place

- Whether you see memory as sacred, spiritual, or simply human, how do you honor the presence of the one you miss?

- What are some of your favorite memories of your child? Write them down in vivid detail.

- Are there certain days, songs, smells, or places that trigger powerful memories?

- How do you want others to remember your child's life?

- How might you create a small ritual or tradition to honor their memory each year?

Chapter 7—When Grief Lives in the Body

- How has your body changed since your loss? What symptoms have you noticed?

- How do you treat yourself on days when your grief feels physical?

- What are gentle, loving practices you can offer your body (rest, nature, breathing, prayer)?

- How does it feel to think of your body as carrying both grief and sacred memory?

Chapter 8—Sacred Rage, Sacred Love: Living Forward with Both

- When you feel rage, what specific memories, injustices, or moments come to mind?

- When you feel love, what memories or emotions rise to the surface?

- How might you honor both your anger and your love without feeling like you have to "fix" or silence either one?

- Write a letter to your child that holds both the rage and the love together.

Chapter 9—The Sacred Work of Living Forward

- In what ways can living forward honor—not replace—the love that still pulses in your soul? What does moving forward mean to you, in your own time and way?

- What does "living forward" look like for you right now? What does it *not* look like?

- In what ways have you changed—emotionally, spiritually, relationally—since your loss?

- What do you want the world to know about your child and how they still impact your life?

- How does your vision of the future look different since your loss—and what does hope now mean to you?

- How will you honor your child's memory in the way you live, love, and serve?

Chapter 10—When the World Moves On Without You

- When was the first time you felt even a moment of happiness after your loss?

- What emotions rose up—joy, guilt, fear, hope?

- How does it feel to think of joy as a way to honor your child's memory, not erase it?

- What small acts of joy could you fight for today, without guilt?

Chapter 11—Fighting for Joy Without Guilt

- How have you experienced others "moving on" before you were ready?

- What emotions rise when you think about the world's expectation for you to be "better" by now?

- How do you honor your child's memory even when others stop mentioning their name?

- What would you say if you could write a letter to the world about grief's timeline?

Sacred Rage Theological Self-Assessment Survey and Interpretive Framework

When the Soul Screams: A Self-Assessment on Grief, Rage, and Divine Protest

Grief does not follow a straight line, and neither does faith. This assessment is not designed to measure how "spiritual" you are or to place you in a fixed category. Rather, it is an invitation to pause and listen—to your soul, your sorrow, your sacred questions. Whether you are reeling from loss, wrestling with God, or simply seeking language for the ache inside you, this tool is here to accompany you—not to diagnose or define you.

Each response is a reflection of where you are today, not where you'll always be. In seasons of suffering, we may feel closer to protest than to praise, and that's okay. The God who welcomed Job's lament and Jeremiah's fury can hold your truth, too. This is a space for honest reflection—for the quiet mourner, the sacred agitator, and the one who longs to be seen in their sorrow.

You are not alone in your questions. And your grief, however it manifests, is holy ground.

Instructions:

Respond to each statement using the scale below:

1—Strongly Disagree

2—Disagree

3—Neutral

4—Agree

5—Strongly Agree

Theology of Grief and Loss

1. I believe grief is a sacred experience, not a sign of weak faith. _____

2. I feel spiritually disoriented when I witness or experience unjust loss. _____

3. I see divine presence in the midst of my suffering. _____

4. I believe questioning God is a valid part of faith. _____

5. I can articulate how loss has reshaped my understanding of God. _____

Sacred Rage and Divine Protest

1. I have felt anger toward God or the universe in times of loss. _____

2. I believe sacred rage is a valid spiritual response to injustice. _____

3. I have expressed anger in ways that felt prayerful or holy. _____

4. I connect with biblical or theological figures who protested divine silence. _____

5. My anger has deepened my spiritual life rather than distanced me from it. _____

Justice, Theodicy, and Meaning-Making

1. I struggle with the idea that "everything happens for a reason." _____

2. I believe not all pain is divinely orchestrated. _____

3. I long for theological frameworks that make room for both grief and protest. _____

4. I see the death of children or innocent lives as a theological dilemma. _____

5. I believe churches should create space for conversations about sacred anger. _____

Integration and Embodied Practice

1. I express grief/rage through creative or spiritual practices (writing, prayer, protest, art). _____

2. I feel more connected to others when I can share my story of loss authentically. _____

3. I believe lament is a form of worship. _____

4. I have found ways to live with unanswered prayers. _____

5. I carry both love and rage without needing one to cancel the other. _____

Scoring and Interpretive Framework

Total Score Range: 20–100

20–39: The Contained Wrestler

You may hold deep emotions but struggle to give them space in your theology. Sacred rage may feel unfamiliar or even threatening. You likely seek more traditional frameworks of comfort but might benefit from permission to grieve honestly and question deeply.

40–59: The Quiet Lamenter

You recognize your grief and have started integrating it into your spirituality, but your sacred anger may still feel suppressed or underexplored. You're beginning to acknowledge the tension between belief and pain and are looking for language to name your inner protest.

60–79: The Holy Agitator

You have experienced grief that shook your theology—and you let it. Sacred rage is not foreign to you; in fact, it may have become part of your prayer life. You wrestle with God, not out of disbelief but out of intimacy.

80–100: The Prophetic Griever

You live at the intersection of lament and liberation. You see sacred rage not as rebellion but as reverence. You protest out of love—for what was lost and for what must change.

Next Steps / Spiritual Reflection Suggestions

- Write a lament in your own voice, without censoring your anger or questions.
- Read Job 3 or Jer 20 aloud and consider what it means to bring rage to the altar.

- Engage in communal storytelling, where sacred grief is honored in the open.

- Consider spiritual direction or theological journaling to explore how your image of God has shifted.

- Ask yourself, "Where is God in my protest? What do I want God to hear from me?"

Full Interpretive Framework

20–39: The Contained Wrestler

You may hold deep emotions but struggle to give them space in your theology. Sacred rage may feel unfamiliar or even threatening. You likely seek more traditional frameworks of comfort but might benefit from permission to grieve honestly and question deeply. You may have been taught that faith requires composure, but your soul may be craving room to express anger and sorrow without shame.

40–59: The Quiet Lamenter

You recognize your grief and have started integrating it into your spirituality, but your sacred anger may still feel suppressed or underexplored. You're beginning to acknowledge the tension between belief and pain and are looking for language to name your inner protest. You carry a quiet grief, and while you seek theological answers, your journey might be less about answers and more about being heard.

60–79: The Holy Agitator

You have experienced grief that shook your theology—and you let it. Sacred rage is not foreign to you; in fact, it may have become part of your prayer life. You wrestle with God, not out of disbelief but out of intimacy. You likely see lament as a form of intercession and advocacy. You are learning to live with contradiction: trust and fury, reverence and resistance. You are finding your voice as a holy agitator.

80–100: The Prophetic Griever

You live at the intersection of lament and liberation. You see sacred rage not as rebellion but as reverence. You protest out of love—for what was lost and for what must change. Your grief is both personal and collective. You carry the weight of injustice with dignity, refusing to numb or spiritualize your pain. You minister through your honesty, embodying a theology that makes space for sacred defiance and divine compassion. Your prophetic grief is not just a cry—it is a call.

Resources for the Journey

Grief does not end with the closing of a book. If you are walking the sacred path of loss, especially after the death of a child or loved one, these resources may help you continue forward with support, language, and community.

Books on Grief and Child Loss

- *Lament for a Son* by Nicholas Wolterstorff
- *It's OK That You're Not OK* by Megan Devine
- *The Year of Magical Thinking* by Joan Didion
- *Permission to Mourn* by Tom Zuba

Grief Support Communities

- **The Compassionate Friends** —www.compassionatefriends.org
- **GriefShare**—www.griefshare.org
- **Option B**—www.optionb.org
- **Me and Grief**—Facebook group led by Rev. Dr. Damien W. D. Davis

Online Healing Spaces

- Podcasts:
    - *Terrible, Thanks for Asking*
    - *The Good Mourning Podcast*
- YouTube Talks:
    - David Kessler (on grief and meaning)
    - Megan Devine's "Speaking Grief" series

📞 Grief and Crisis Hotlines

- **Suicide and Crisis Lifeline (USA): 988 or 1-800-273-TALK (8255)**
- **National Alliance for Children's Grief: www.childrengrieve.org**
- **NAMI Helpline: 1-800-950-NAMI (6264)**

You are not alone. This journey is sacred. May these tools walk beside you in silence, in weeping, in rage, and in remembering.

About the Author

Reverend Dr. Damien W. D. Davis is a theologian, chaplain, author, and grief companion whose work is rooted in the sacred intersection of spiritual care and lived experience. A native of Chicago's South Side, he is a proud graduate of Wilberforce University—the nation's first privately owned HBCU—where he earned his bachelor of arts in mass media / communications with a minor in religious studies. While at Wilberforce, he served as second vice president of the Student Government Association, laying early foundations for a life devoted to community leadership and faith-rooted justice.

He later earned his master of divinity (MDiv) and doctor of ministry (DMin) degrees from McCormick Theological Seminary, where his doctoral research focused on pastoral care training for prison chaplains. That work earned him the prestigious John Randall Hunt Prize for Outstanding Doctor of Ministry Thesis. He has completed multiple units of clinical pastoral education and holds certification from the National Catholic Bioethics Center.

Dr. Davis is also the author of *Prison Life and the Aftermath of Thug Living*, a bold and compassionate narrative on transformation beyond incarceration. He has served in diverse ministry settings—from hospice chaplaincy with Harmony Cares to providing spiritual care in maximum-security penitentiaries. He is currently a staff chaplain at Franciscan Health and Lurie

Children's Hospital, offering presence and spiritual support to patients and families in moments of crisis.

He is a member of Trinity United Church of Christ in Chicago, where his faith continues to be nurtured in a community committed to justice, liberation, and radical love. He also leads *Me and Grief*, a vibrant and compassionate online support group on Facebook where individuals journey through loss together. With heartfelt reflections, weekly devotionals, and a sacred space for vulnerability, *Me and Grief* has become a lifeline for those who are learning to live forward while honoring their pain.

Whether sitting with the bereaved, speaking in classrooms or pulpits, or walking alongside families in grief, Dr. Davis brings both pastoral tenderness and prophetic honesty. His life's work is a testimony to sacred defiance—declaring that love does not end at the grave, and grief deserves reverence, not resolution.

He is a devoted husband to Sharon Okoh-Davis and father to Josiah, Macy, and Brooklyn—forever Boogie—whose light did not go out but multiplied.

Bibliography

Bonnheim, Ana. "Everything You Need to Know About the Jewish Custom of Shiva." ReformJudaism.org. https://reformjudaism.org/beliefs-practices/lifecycle-rituals/death-mourning/everything-you-need-know-about-jewish-custom-shiva.

Coogan, Michael David, et al., eds. *The New Oxford Annotated Bible: New Revised Standard Version with the Apocrypha; An Ecumenical Study Bible.* 4th ed. Oxford: Oxford University Press, 2010.

Danker, Frederick W., et al. *A Greek-English Lexicon of the New Testament and Other Early Christian Literature.* 3rd ed. Chicago: University of Chicago Press, 2000.

The Editors of *Encyclopedia Britannica.* "Shraddha." *Encyclopedia Britannica,* last updated Mar. 16, 2024. https://www.britannica.com/topic/shraddha.

Haute Hijab. "The Islamic Perspective on Grief—Coping with Individual and Community Loss/Hardship." Haute Hijab, Aug. 23, 2019. https://blog.hautehijab.com/post/islamic-perspective-on-grief.

Keener, Craig S. *The Gospel of John: A Commentary.* Vol. 1. Peabody: Hendrickson, 2003.

Lion's Roar. "How Buddhism Helps Us Understand Grief." Lion's Roar. https://www.lionsroar.com/buddhism/grief/.

O'Connor, Mary-Frances. *The Grieving Body: How the Stress of Loss Can Be an Opportunity for Healing.* New York: HarperCollins, 2025.

Saheeh International, trans. *The Qur'an: English Meanings.* Abul-Qasim, 1997.

Story, Karen. "A Burial in West Africa." Order of the Good Death, Apr. 20, 2016. https://www.orderofthegooddeath.com/article/a-burial-in-west-africa/.

www.ingramcontent.com/pod-product-compliance
Lightning Source LLC
Chambersburg PA
CBHW060420090426
42734CB00011B/2380